Decision Making in Social

Decision Making in Social Work

Decision Making in Social Work

Terence O'Sullivan

palgrave

Published by
PALGRAVE
Houndmills, Basingstoke, Hampshire RG21 6XS and
175 Fifth Avenue, New York, N.Y. 10010
Companies and representatives throughout the world

PALGRAVE is the new global academic imprint of
St. Martin's Press LLC Scholarly and Reference Division and
Palgrave Publishers Ltd (formerly Macmillan Press Ltd).

ISBN 0–333–68481–8

This book is printed on paper suitable for recycling and
made from fully managed and sustained forest sources.

A catalogue record for this book is available
from the British Library.

10   9   8   7   6   5   4   3   2
09   08   07   06   05   04   03   02   01

Copy-edited and typeset by Povey–Edmondson
Tavistock and Rochdale, England

Printed in Malaysia

To Bryony, Joseph, Alice and Ryan

Contents

List of Figures

Acknowledgements

I would like to thank Tom Strickland, Leonne Griggs and Marie Ramsden for their encouraging comments on an early draft of the book and Norma Baldwin for valuable suggestions on ways in which the book could be more clearly focused on practice. Particular thanks is due to Robert Adams who gave me critical feedback at all stages, from the very beginning to the final draft and for his generous support and guidance throughout; to Tony Petch for his comments on the first two chapters; to the staff and students of the University of Lincolnshire and Humberside who over the years have participated in the unit of the same title and, often unknowingly, have helped in the generation of the ideas contained within the book. Last and not least the anonymous Macmillan reviewers whose comments promoted the book's development. Although a number of people have contributed to the book's improvement, the responsibility for its content is mine alone.

TERENCE O'SULLIVAN

Introduction

When a child is killed by his or her parents, a passer-by murdered by a mentally disordered person or the dead body of an older person has lain undetected in their dingy flat for weeks, the social workers involved are often accused of errors of judgement or incompetence. Sometimes this criticism may be warranted, but often it is unfounded, appearing to fulfil a need to hold somebody responsible for the failings of society. Subsequent attempts to improve social work decision making can be divided into two categories: those that endeavour to de-professionalise social work by creating procedures for social workers to follow and those that endeavour to strengthen professional social work by developing its knowledge and skills base. This book falls into the latter category and is rooted in the belief that the complexity of social situations means that procedures alone cannot determine what social workers do.

There are a number of sources of complexity in social work decision making that require knowledge, analysis and high levels of skill. Social workers need to take into account interacting factors operating on different levels, ranging from the personal to the societal. Each client and his or her situation is unique and when a decision is actually being made it is not possible to predict the outcome with certainty. If social workers could always play it safe, this uncertainty would be less of a problem but the damage and injustice caused would be unacceptable even to social work's fiercest critics. There is also the need to involve clients and other stakeholders in the making of decisions, something made more complicated by them not necessarily sharing the same interests; for example, what is in the interests of carers may not always be in the interest of the people being cared for.

To manage this complexity a professional practice framework is needed rather than bureaucratic procedures and technical rules. The term 'framework' is used to denote a supporting structure of grouped concepts and ideas, placed in relation to each other with the purpose of providing a map that social workers can use to order their minds and act with purpose and clarity in the situations they face. Such a framework needs to embody the complex features of decision making in social work, such as recognising that social work decision making is not clear cut but involves difficult issues of practice. Decision making is not a single skill but a complex cluster of skills including thinking skills, interpersonal skills and political skills, concerned with processes at micro, intermediate and macro levels. Within the framework the various interacting elements need to be fitted together by taking a holistic perspective requiring a synthesising approach which integrates disparate material from a wide range of subject areas. The resulting synthesis may not always be to the satisfaction of the specialists working in contributory fields of study.

The framework is set out in the nine chapters of this book, with Chapter 1 laying the necessary groundwork by exploring the issues raised by a focus on the making of decisions in social work. Chapter 2 considers the contexts that need to be taken into account when making a decision. The next two chapters focus on the interpersonal and political domains, with Chapter 3 discussing the involvement of clients and Chapter 4 discussing the stakeholders meeting together. Chapter 5 explores the more internal processes of thinking and feeling in decision making. Chapters 6 and 7 look at two central aspects of decision making, framing of the decision situation (Chapter 6) and how the choice of options can be made (Chapter 7). Chapter 8 considers the evaluation of decision making, decision implementation and decision outcome. Finally, Chapter 9 concludes the book by considering why sound decision making does not always lead to good outcomes.

People tend to relate more easily to concrete examples rather than abstract ideas, but abstract ideas are necessary in order to transfer knowledge and skill between different situations. A balance can be achieved by using concrete examples to illustrate abstract ideas so as to facilitate understanding of the issues involved. To this end an illustrative example is used in each chapter, but the reader needs to treat these with caution. The illustrative examples should not be considered as case studies of practice, since they fall far short of giving a full account of the decision making in the situations outlined. They focus on particular points in time and particular decisions, whereas decision making – as stressed above – invariably involves a continuous process of a series of decisions taken over time. While the framework is intended to be a general one applicable across the broad range of social work, in trying to make the chapters more accessible, they inevitably have come to reflect the particular concerns of the case examples. The eight case examples do not comprehensively represent the full range of fields and activities to be found within social work. Where specific courses of action have been identified, they have been chosen to illustrate particular points, not examples of good or bad practice.

It also needs to be remembered that the purpose of the following chapters is not to examine the issues of the specific fields of social work, from which the illustrative examples are drawn, but to explore the particular aspect of the decision making framework that forms the subject-matter of that chapter. For example, the purpose of Chapter 1 is not to examine child protection investigations, which happens to be the illustrative example, but to lay the groundwork for building a framework for decision making in social work. In this way the different aspects of decision making in social work are considered chapter by chapter so that by the end of the book the framework of decision making in social work will be complete. Practice issues such as oppression and anti-oppressive practice are integrated throughout the framework as a whole, but the index can be used to identify particular points where more detailed expositions are given.

1

Making Decisions

Although decision making is generally regarded as an important area of professional expertise, it has been somewhat overlooked as a specific focus in social work. This comparative neglect necessitates the ground being prepared before being able to discuss the first aspect of the decision making framework in Chapter 2. This groundwork will be done by addressing the following questions. Why focus on decision making? What has prevented a clear focus on decision making in social work? What does decision making in social work involve? What is sound decision making?

ILLUSTRATIVE EXAMPLE

One Friday afternoon, an anonymous telephone call is received at a local social services department office claiming that a four-year-old child has been badly beaten by her parents at a particular address. The office had received a number of such anonymous calls recently, which on investigation turned out to be hoaxes. The two duty social workers, unable to find out any further information about the family, consult with their team manager and police colleagues. Together they decide that the best way of proceeding is to carry out a home visit as a preliminary enquiry, to see if there are any grounds for a full investigation. At the address the two social workers identify themselves to a young woman who answers the door. They establish that she is the mother of a four-year-old child who is asleep upstairs. They explain about the allegation made by the anonymous caller and ask to see the child. At this point the woman becomes indignant, stating that she was not going to let them wake her daughter just because of some malicious caller and slams the door. The two social workers return to their car to decide what to do next.

Why Focus on Decision Making?

Child protection agencies receive referrals from a variety of sources concerning children who may need protection from harm, some of which will be filtered out very quickly, while others will be further investigated (Gibbons, Conroy and Bell, 1995, p. 51). One of the many problems faced by these agencies is how to respond to the small percentage of referrals from members of the public who do not give their name. The majority of these will turn out to require no further action, but need careful screening as calls of this nature do at times contain important information (Wattam, 1995, p. 172). They also require sensitive handling, as being implicated in harming your child, even without any foundation, is a traumatic experience for families. A number of decisions have already been made in the illustrative example and the social workers now need to decide whether to call at the house again in the hope that the woman has calmed down or to return to the office to discuss other ways to get to see the child. The processes involved in deciding what to do can remain ill defined and focusing on them entails bringing these into sharp relief. Given the relative neglect of decision making by social work academics and practitioners, the justification of this focus may need to be made explicit. In what follows, it will be argued that decision making is a core activity in social work that needs particular attention to sharpen awareness of the issues involved and so enable professional practice to be recognised and developed.

Decision making as a core activity in social work

Much of what social workers do concerns decisions about future courses of actions (Banks, 1995, p. 9), which puts decision making at the heart of social work as a core professional activity. All the various tasks involved in social work processes, no matter how they are divided, involve the making of decisions. This includes referral/allocation, enquiry/investigation/assessment, planning, plan implementation, review and closure decisions. If social workers are to increase the chances of achieving their professional aims of promoting human welfare, social justice and preventing human suffering, the decisions made within social work will need careful attention. The distinctive features of this key generic skill will need to be articulated if a purposeful, accountable and sound social work practice is to be developed, that would more fully take into account the tensions and contradictions within social work.

Social work decisions are often problematic balancing acts, based on incomplete information, within time constraints, under pressure from different sources, with uncertainty as to the likely outcome of the different options, and the constant fear that something will go wrong and the social worker will be blamed. To be able to find their way through this labyrinth, social workers need to be critically aware of the processes involved so as to be able to proactively participate and not be swept along by events. If the two social workers in the car that Friday afternoon do not systematically think through the decision situation and the options available to them, there is a danger that a child will be further harmed or, alternatively, that an innocent family will be traumatised by an unwarranted child protection investigation. If decisions are not carefully considered, with the whole situation taken into account, opportunities to promote human welfare may be lost or human suffering caused.

The sharpening of awareness of issues of practice

A focus on decision making can sharpen awareness and understanding of issues of practice and so make improvements possible. For example, the issues of how to counteract oppression have been the subject of much debate within social work. These can be brought into sharper relief by viewing them from the point of view of decision making. Within Dalrymple and Burke's influential (1995) work on anti-oppressive practice there is a recognition that 'the professional responsibilities of social workers can be implemented oppressively or in an empowering way' (Payne, 1997b, p. 258). Decision making becomes a source of oppression when power is misused or abused, but careful attention to how decisions are made will enable these issues of power to be confronted head-on. Oppression can be defined as a person or people being kept down or restricted in some way, resulting in harm, hardship, suffering or injustice. Anti-oppressive practice endeavours to counteract oppression, whether its source is aspects of the social worker's own practice, agency policies or the structure of the society in which the client lives. Decision making can be either a potential source of oppression or an opportunity to work in an anti-oppressive manner.

In the context of multicultural societies there is the potential danger of social workers and other professional workers being ethnocentric in their approach. This is particularly important in the relationship between members of the majority ethnic group and members of minority ethnic groups. Decision making involves framing the decision situation – a process that highlights the problem of cultural bias (see Chapter 6). The danger is that the basis of a decision can be the implicit and uncritical cultural understandings acquired through ongoing processes of socialisation and internalisation – for example, when the supposed defects of a different culture are focused on rather than its strengths (Ahmed, 1986, p. 141). Explicitly focusing on decision making and the way decision situations are framed can promote critical self-awareness of cultural beliefs and the influence these can have in the making of decisions. In this way the development of an ethnically sensitive and anti-racist social work can be linked to the way social workers make decisions.

Another example of the way focusing on decision making can improve social work practice is by promoting client involvement in the making of decisions. Partnership has become a popular idea and is increasingly seen as a way of reconciling or managing the contradictions within social work. Yet the notion of partnership has often been used in a vague and indiscriminate way to denote a general idea of working together. Placed within a decision making framework, partnership can be clearly distinguished from other levels of involvement (see Chapter 3), giving a greater chance of it being achieved in practice. Within a decision making framework, partnership can be characterised as negotiating decisions rather than imposing them or empowering clients to take control. Partnership has often been presented as a more favourable approach than paternalism (Calder, 1995), but a more complex framework is needed that will show that sometimes partnership may not be feasible, while at others it may not be desirable. It may not be feasible when making decisions concerned with the risk of harm to others or desirable when clients are making their own life decisions.

A positive response to criticisms of practice

The image social workers have of themselves impacts on how they approach their work, and can determine whether they have con-fidence in their ability as professional workers to make the best decisions possible in uncertain and complex situations or whether they defensively hide behind rules and procedures. Agency and government responses to the shortcomings of social work practice, sometimes found by official inquiries, have tended to undermine professional practice by taking the form of the creation or modification of guidelines and procedures. Although these can provide a valuable focus for professional social work, they can only be a guide in the face of complex situations. This is something recognised by the inquiries themselves. For example, the inquiry report into the death of Tyra Henry at the hands of her father states that doing 'everything by the book would more probably have shut out than have stimulated' the sensitivity and imagination the management of Tyra's protection required (London Borough of Lambeth, 1987, p.102). Professional practice itself needs to be developed by focusing on areas of professional expertise and becoming clearer about what these involve. One aspect of this development is the way social workers conceptualise decision making as an activity and their need for a conceptual map of the many different interconnected aspects involved. To successfully manage this complex activity, an understanding of how the different aspects connect with each other is required, giving recognition to decision making as a multifaceted professional activity operating on a number of different levels.

The image others have of social workers is as important as the image social workers have of themselves. The response of the mass media to tragic deaths and various scandals has often been to pillory social workers for not doing their job properly (see Franklin and Parton, 1991; Aldridge, 1994). In these circumstances it has been difficult to counteract the dominant negative images of social workers being incompetent. Images such as social workers failing to protect children from abusing parents or destroying families by unjustified removal of children or the uncaring failure to meet the obvious needs of an older person discharged from hospital, or failing to recognise the high risk a mentally disordered person poses to his family. Although no profession is beyond criticism, much of the negative comment on social work has been ill-informed, with social workers becoming scapegoats for the ills of society.

In order to put the record straight, the social work profession needs to be able to clearly explain the nature of social work decision making to the public and mass media to promote a more informed view which appreciates the uncertainty and contradictions social workers face at the time decisions are actually taken. By focusing on decision making, social workers can become more articulate in their justification of the judgements they make. This can be achieved, for example, by explaining that social work decisions need to be judged on the basis of what was known at the time the decision was made and that social workers are often endeavouring to balance the contradictory demands placed upon them by society. An illustration of this is provided by the chapter example in which the two social workers do not want to intrude unnecessarily into family life but at the same time want to ensure a child is not being harmed. They endeavour to achieve a balance based on the information they have. When the uncertainty has ended and the facts become known it is relatively easy to look back with the benefit of hindsight and say it should have been obvious that it was a hoax call or, alternatively, that it should have been obvious that this caller expressed a justified concern.

What Has Prevented a Clear Focus on Decision Making

Given the arguments put forward in the previous section it may be surprising that to date decision making has not received more attention within social work practice, social work education and social work theory. There has been no book devoted to social work decision making and key texts have largely failed to explicitly focus on this crucial aspect of practice. A number of barriers can be identified that have contributed in different ways to decision making being somewhat overlooked.

Curriculum barriers: the organisation of knowledge in social work

The curriculum of a subject puts a boundary around what is regarded as relevant knowledge. Curricula tend to be organised into compartments or units and the relationship between these units can be open or closed (see Bernstein, 1971, p. 49). Leaving aside the contested nature of the knowledge base of social work, there are a number of ways of dividing up the social work curriculum. Social work students may study social work values, social work skills and social work theory. Alternatively the focus may be on the different aspects of the social work process, in whatever terms it is conceived – for example, assessment, planning and intervention. Subjects may be divided into service areas such as adult care services and child care services or topic areas such as child abuse, elder abuse or mental health, or knowledge areas like social work law or organisational theory or life course studies. It is not uncommon for all these ways of dividing the curriculum to be used in conjunction with each other. However, the subject-matter of this book has tended *not* to be considered systematically under the heading *decision making in social work* but rather spread around the curriculum in a fragmented way.

Emotional barriers: avoidance of responsibility

The comparative neglect of decision making is all the more surprising given that an integral part of social work is the management of tensions, contradictions and uncertainties. Social workers often find themselves in a position of 'damned if I do and damned if I don't'. Caught between contradictory demands, they often feel like 'piggy in the middle' (Clarke, 1993, p. 19): for example, trying to ensure children are protected from harm while respecting the responsibilities of parents or trying to ensure that adult needs are met while keeping within the budget. The social workers involved with the Carlile family before Kimberley Carlile was tragically killed by her stepfather were criticised for not insisting that they saw Kimberley (London Borough of Greenwich, 1992), yet the social workers who suspected a group of Orkney children were being sexually abused were criticised for not being cautious enough when they removed the children (Clyde, 1992). Part of the neglect of decision making can be seen as a way to avoid the explicit consideration of the internal conflicts that social workers inevitably experience.

Given the tensions, contradictions and uncertainties of social work, it is not surprising that there is a certain amount of ambivalence towards decision making. Even though the responsibility for making judgements is a welcome basis for professional identity, it may also be felt to be an emotional and political burden. Social workers often correctly judge that none of the available options will lead to a satisfactory outcome and there are times when the practitioner may prefer to turn away from the responsibility for making decisions. At these times it is more comfortable to see others as making the decisions; the responsibility is being displaced onto managers, administrators, lawyers, doctors, clients, magistrates or judges. Giving attention to decision making is a potential source of anxiety as it identifies the need to come to terms with making decisions on incomplete information with no certainty as to their impact. Focusing on decision making highlights the fallible nature of human decision making, with the human capacity to process information being strictly limited (Hogarth, 1987). Decisions are not always taken on a reasoned basis (Zey, 1992), with a danger that rules of thumb and short cuts are used (Kahneman, Slovic and Tversky, 1982). Research shows that people have difficulty in explaining how they make particular decisions (Carroll and Johnson, 1990) and given the life-and-death nature of some decisions within social work, highlighting the limitations of human decision making is potentially disconcerting.

Ideological barriers: tensions between different views of social work

Over the decades there have been tensions and struggles within social work which can be characterised in a number of ways, one of which is as between three views of the social worker: the social worker as a professional worker who makes professional judgements; the social worker as an agency functionary who follows procedures; and the social worker as social activist who endeavours to bring about social justice. The tensions and struggles have never been fully resolved and all three views are part of the inheritance of present-day social work, although during particular periods of its history one view may have been more prominent than the others. The three views of social work share a common uneasiness about decision making, but for differing reasons.

There are many strands to professional work (Payne, 1996), one of which emphasises clients as decision makers, with rights and responsibilities to determine their own futures. A focus on decision making can be mistakenly seen as going against this principle, even though such a focus does *not* mean social workers take decisions for their clients. A similar misunderstanding can occur with the principle of being non-judgemental, which endeavours to avoid negative judgements based on blame and stereotypes. Such negative judgements are unrelated to the use of professional judgement, but there is a potential source of confusion with a possibility that being non-judgemental is interpreted as not making professional judgements. Invoking the principles of client self-determination or non-judgementality will not relieve the social workers, in the example, of making a professional judgement about what to do next.

The view of social workers as agency functionaries locates responsibility for decision making with the government and agency management. According to this view, social workers do not have to concern themselves with the making of professional judgements but should just follow instructions and procedures. Such an approach would alleviate the need to take problematic decisions with the added advantage that if things go wrong the rules can be blamed. Within such a view, the social workers in our example only have to look in their procedural manual to see what to do next. Obviously, such an approach fails to recognise the inevitable limitations of government guidelines and agency procedures and the necessity for social workers as front-line workers to use their discretion and make difficult professional judgements. What the two workers in the car decide to do is a matter of fine judgement, that will depend on the specific circumstances while taking into account agency procedures and guidelines. Instructions and procedures can never take the place of these fine judgements and attempts to make them do so would lead to many errors and damaging clumsy interventions.

The view of social workers as social activists involves a belief that the power to make decisions should be individually and collectively with clients. Within this view, a focus on decision making can be seen as undermining client decision making and diverting attention away from the need to change an unfair system that is the root cause of the problems clients face. Although decision making is correctly associated with the exercise of power, it is only through awareness and skills in decision making that social workers can become effective in empowering people to make decisions about their own lives and bring about social change. Decision making needs to be a key issue in the empowerment of clients and a shying away from it will not promote the redistribution of power that is necessary if clients are to have their rightful place as decision makers.

Each of the three views forms an integral part of social work, which together form its inherent tensions that need to be managed. These tensions involve the three sides of the triangle formed by the main participant groups: clients, managers and professional workers. The unfolding of these tensions is manifested in the changing nature of social work organisations, the scope of the personal social services and the nature of professional social work. The view of social workers as members of a profession recognises that social workers work in a world of uncertainties about which they need to make professional judgements. The view of social workers as functionaries following procedures recognises that social workers are regulated by laws, official guidance and agency procedures. The view of social workers as social activists recognises that many clients lack power and influence in decision making. It is only through an integrative critical awareness of decision making processes and the development of anti-oppressive decision making skills, that social workers can make a realistic attempt to manage these tensions.

What Does Decision Making in Social Work Involve?

Decision making in social work is problematic from a number of points of view. At a very basic level it is difficult to define and recognise what decision making is and explain what it involves. This necessitates setting out a conceptual map of related ideas and concepts that provides a means of identifying and analysing decision making.

What is decision making?

Decision making will be defined as the process of *making* a choice where the emphasis is on making, that is constructing, a choice. Decision making occurs where there is some degree of recognition of a need or a desire to make a choice. It would be relatively straightforward to confine decision making to *deliberation about the decision situation in order to make a choice*, if it were not for the fact that some choices are intuitive and are made without conscious thought. These non-deliberated intuitive decisions are particularly important in social work (England, 1986) and will be discussed at some length in Chapter 5. Such decisions are based on expertise built up through experience and should not be confused with an unthinking reaction which has no sound basis. Notwithstanding the importance of intuitive decisions in professional work, deliberation is a key idea within the framework when decision situations require careful analysis.

Decision making varies in a number of important ways. Firstly, decisions vary as to how much deliberation they are given; some decisions being given extensive deliberation, whereas others are made with scant deliberation and others still no deliberation at all, as in the case of intuitive decisions. Very little progress would be made if social workers were to analyse every decision in detail, but on the other hand there are certain decision points that justify detailed consideration of the different options. Secondly, decisions vary in the degree of awareness the decision maker has of making a choice. At times the decision maker can be very conscious of the fact that they are making a choice, while at other times they may have minimal awareness that a choice is being made. Thirdly, decisions also vary as to their perceived consequences and so the amount of pressure experienced. Some decisions are viewed as important because, for example, they are perceived to have life and death consequences, whereas others are considered relatively unimportant because they are thought to have minimal consequences.

Decision chains

Although there are well-recognised decision points, such as reviews, for the most part it is difficult to delineate where decision making starts and finishes. Rather than thinking of decision making having a clear beginning and end, it is more appropriate to think in terms of chains of decisions taken over time, each feeding into the next. The analogy of a chain will be used despite the dangers of such an analogy being taken too far. The links in the chain can be thought of as the choices made, the chain starting at the point of referral and ending at the point the case file is closed, as shown in Figure 1.1. The construction of the chain takes the decision situation in a particular direction either in incremental steps or by making major changes. The illustrative examples used in this book feature particular points in time within particular decision chains. In this chapter's example, the chain is at the enquiry stage, a number of decisions have already been made and after the two social workers have decided what to do, others will follow.

Whose decision?

When considering decision making in social work, there is a danger that only the decisions taken by social workers will be focused on. It is important to remember that different people have different roles

FIGURE 1.1   *Decision chains in social work*

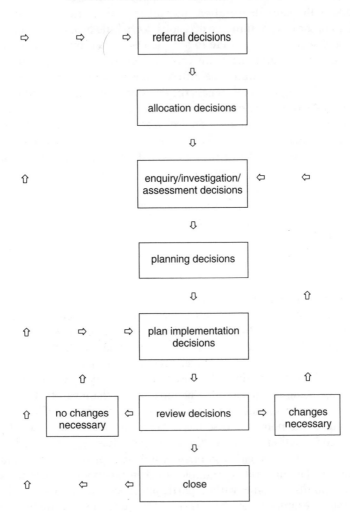

and perspectives to take within a chain of decisions. In the example, the social workers are only two of the stakeholders in the situation. There are a number of other potential stakeholders – including the members of the family, the person who made the anonymous call, the receptionist who took the call, the team manager, the health visitor, the GP, the staff at the nursery school and the police. Each has had, or potentially will have, decisions to make at various points in time. It is important to be clear that within the decision making framework there is no presumption that the social worker makes all the decisions. The focus is the decisions made within social work and the subject-matter is just as much the decisions of clients and the other stakeholders. For this reason the terms *decision maker* or *decision makers* will be used to denote the people who are directly involved in making the actual decision. In a particular situation it is a matter of judgement and negotiation as to who these are, which may be a matter of dispute and conflict between the stakeholders.

The stakeholders

The term *stakeholder* will be used to denote all those who have some interest or concern in the decision being made. It is not an entirely satisfactory term and its potential for being misunderstood has been increased by its association with 'the stakeholder idea' (Jones Finer, 1997, p. 155) of New Labour. Nevertheless it remains the most suitable term available and is used to denote the wide range of people that can have some interest in the making of a decision. This interest will vary in nature, sometimes being a professional or agency interest, while with others it will be a personal, family or life interest. Sometimes the interest will be intense and central, as with the child alleged to have been abused, while at other times it may be more marginal and circumscribed, as with the receptionist who took the anonymous telephone call. Stakeholders will also vary as to the power position they occupy in society and in relation to the agencies involved, with some being in a relatively powerful position, while others may be relatively powerless. Not all the stakeholders will necessarily be decision makers – others could be providers of information or services. The term *client* will be used to denote the stakeholder in the centre of the decision situation. It is used here in the absence of a more suitable alternative with no connotation of dependency or passivity and in the knowledge that it has been the subject of considerable criticism (for example, see Brown and Bourne, 1996, pp. 67–8).

The decision situation

The term *decision situation* will be used as a shorthand to denote the totality of circumstances that require or prompt a decision and is employed in preference to *decision problem* which suggests a much narrower focus. The decision situation includes the different contexts and the various stakeholders, placing appropriate emphasis on holism and inclusiveness, with it being particularly important that all aspects of the decision situation are considered from the micro level to the macro level and its development over time. The decision situation is in a constant state of development and the picture that decision makers have needs to be continually updated and kept under review. According to Radford (1989, pp. 9–12), well-structured decision situations can be resolved by a specific procedure, whereas ill-structured decision situations are those in which people 'may disagree about the nature of a particular situation and the manner in which it is to be treated'. The difference between professional and procedural approaches to decision making in social work can be seen as a dispute over the nature of the decision situations encountered within social work.

The social worker's role

Social workers' involvement in the making of decisions is complex and can take a number of different forms depending on the circumstances of the decision situation. It is not surprising that there can be confusion over the role social workers have, as it can change between and within decision situations. At any particular point in time social workers need to be clear as to what their role is. Four distinct roles can be identified:

- facilitation of client decision making;
- making professional judgements;
- collaborative decision making in partnership with others (including clients, other professionals/agencies, colleagues and managers);
- making recommendations to others or being consulted by others (including managers, courts and panels).

These are not mutually exclusive but rather different aspects of the social work role. The facilitation of client decision making is included in the framework, despite this sometimes being treated as a separate and distinct casework activity (for example, see McClam and Woodside, 1994).

Circumscribing social work decision making

Where to draw the boundary around social work decision making is problematic. On the one hand it is possible to argue that the focus should be on decisions made by social workers within front-line social work. On the other hand it can also be argued that the focus should include the less visible decisions (often taken outside social work) that shape the decision making agenda. The first is rejected as too restricted, given the central place of client empowerment and interdisciplinary co-operation, while the second would tend to take the focus away from micro case decisions of social work to the more macro policy decisions of social policy. The legitimate fear in restricting the focus to case decisions is that the important question, 'Who set the decision making agenda and prevented other issues being focused on?', will not be asked. The decisional agenda in social work is in danger of being too restrictive, focusing on narrow concerns shaped elsewhere by the decision making and non-decision making of governments and multinational corporations. Non-decision making is a term used by Bachrach and Baratz (1962) to denote activities that prevent issues from surfacing for decision. Widening the focus to include this dimension is beyond the scope of the present decision making framework, that needs to be put alongside a wider social analysis of who has power in society.

Social workers can be accused of too readily accepting the decision making agenda as set by powerful others and not tackling the social issues that underlie the problems clients face. In many situations social workers, clients and the other stakeholders have limited influence over what the actual decision making agenda is (Dominelli, 1997a, p. 115). This is particularly so in terms of the absence of certain issues, for example, the eradication of poverty. It can be argued that stakeholders do not fully or effectively use the influence they do have or put enough energy into increasing their influence but, as in the chapter example, the decision making agenda has been set by the government, the social workers' agency and possibly the mass media. According to this agenda the social workers have been constrained to frame their work narrowly as one of child protection and not as, for example, more generally as promoting the overall welfare of children (Otway, 1996). If the child in the example is found to be safe but living in poverty the chances are that this will not become the focus of action. Unfortunately agencies can restrict their duties under the Children Act to safeguard and promote the welfare of children who are in need, by narrowly defining what is to count as need. The framework endeavours to take account of the agenda-setting level by being critically aware of the contexts in which decisions are made but it is mostly beyond the scope of day-to-day social work practice to directly change these contexts. Changing these contexts is more the collective concern of social work, in which individual social workers have a duty to participate. An important part of social work is to endeavour to influence the wider social issues through the individual and collective activities of social workers and clients in relation to agencies, governments and the general public.

What is Sound Decision Making?

Process and outcome are often contrasted with each other but both are important aspects of decision making, with a distinction being made between a sound decision and an effective decision. Sound decision making concerns *process,* with a *sound decision* being one that has been *made* appropriately. Of course, what is regarded as appropriate is open to question but will be delineated as one in which the decision makers have:

- been critically aware of and taken into account the decision making contexts;
- involved the client to the highest feasible level;
- consulted with the stakeholders;
- been clear in their thinking and aware of their emotions;
- produced a well-reasoned frame of the decision situation that is consistent with the available information; and
- based their course of action on a systematic appraisal of the options.

An *effective decision* is one that achieves the decision makers' goals and so is concerned with the *decision outcome*. Sound decision making increases the chances of decisions being effective; however, given the uncertain and complex nature of social situations this often cannot be ensured. The notion of effective decisions will be returned to in Chapter 8 when the evaluation of decision outcomes will be considered, while the six aspects of sound decision making listed above are fully presented in Chapters 2 to 7, but previewed below in terms of the issues faced by the two social workers.

Taking into account the contexts

In considering how best to pursue their professional aim of promoting human welfare and preventing human suffering, the social workers will need to be critically aware of any relevant legal requirements and agency procedures. They are particularly aware of the limitation of a narrow legalistic procedural approach and endeavour to take a more holistic perspective. They have an in-depth knowledge of the relevant law and know that there is a statutory duty to investigate where they 'have reasonable cause to suspect that a child ... is suffering, or likely to suffer, significant harm' (Children Act, 1989, Section 47(1)(b)). Government guidance is clear that if they do have reasonable cause to suspect, they are 'required to take steps which are reasonably practicable either to obtain acess to the child themselves, or to ensure that access to him [sic] is obtained on their behalf by someone who is authorised by them for a purpose' (Department of Health, 1989a p. 61). The nature of the call and its context has caused the social workers to be cautious; they want more information before deciding whether a joint investigation with the police is warranted. Their team manager and police regard the current status of their work as a preliminary enquiry to gather information but at present they are being thwarted by the mother in their information gathering. Neither the law nor the agency procedures give specific guidance about what to do next in the particular situation.

Involving the client

The social workers in the example regard the unseen child as their primary client and the mother as a secondary client. The difference between primary and secondary clients will be discussed in Chapter 3 but the terms do not necessarily indicate who is the main focus of face-to-face work. The framework includes four levels of involvement – being told, being consulted, being a partner and being in control. If the level of involvement was to be *being told*, the social workers would insist on seeing the child with the aid of a court order if necessary. If it was *being consulted*, the social workers would speak to the mother again, listen to what she had to say and take this into account in making the decision. If the level was *being a partner*, the social workers would negotiate with the mother until they both could agree on a course of action. Finally, if the level of involvement was *being in control* it would be the mother, in possession of all the information, who would decide what to do. A key issue for the social workers is to fit the level of involvement to the nature of the particular decision situation.

Consulting the stakeholders

One issue for the two social workers is who the stakeholders are and how they should be consulted. At this particular point in time, within the series of decisions of the illustrative example, many of the potential stakeholders are unknown to the social workers. There could be a health visitor, a nursery teacher or grandparents that have an appropriate interest in the decision situation. Nevertheless the social workers have consulted a number of stakeholders before they left the office – their team manager and the police – and may now feel a further consultation is necessary. They have spoken to the mother and are trying to gain access to the child. Particular emphasis is given in Chapter 4 to the stakeholders meeting together, which is only likely to happen in the case example if it develops in such a way that a child protection conference becomes appropriate (Department of Health, 1991a, p. 41).

Thinking and feeling about the decision situation

The two social workers' professional intuition tells them that the referral was another malicious call, but they consider whether it is a decision that should be the subject of detailed analysis. They do not want to be either too hasty in dismissing the call as a hoax or in asking for police assistance. They are aware that involving the police, at this stage, may spiral into getting an order to gain entry to the property, possibly with the use of force. The ability of the two social workers to think clearly and vigilantly may be affected by their emotions, and the stress and the exhaustion they are both experiencing. They feel compassion for the woman who opened the door and was obviously shocked and angry about their intrusion. They have had a busy and harrowing week and were looking forward to the weekend; now they find themselves experiencing internal conflict. On the one hand they do not want to subject the mother to further intrusion, but on the other they need to establish that the child is safe.

Framing the decision situation

Through framing processes the available information is shaped and organised into a picture of the situation, decision goals and a set of options. The two social workers endeavour to list the key factors of the situation and consider what weight to give to the fact that most of the anonymous calls the office receives are unfounded. They consider their shorter-term decision goal to be to see the child, in the context of the longer-term goal of promoting the child's overall development within her family. The two social workers consider how they should frame the immediate options and think in terms of two possible courses of action, using as much professional skill as they can muster to persuade the mother to allow them to see the child or return to the office to consult the team manager and police about the possibility of getting a court order.

Choosing an option

The two social workers can base their decision on an appraisal of the set of options identified within their decision frame, alongside the identified key factors and decision goals. The basis could either be a matter of deontological principle – for example, their duty is to see the child no matter how traumatic for the family – or a question of which option is considered most likely to give the best chance of a good outcome or the compassion they feel for the mother. The social workers endeavour in making their choice, to balance the risk of using up more valuable time in the vain attempt to persuade the mother to let them see the child and in the process aggravate her further and the danger of being unnecessarily heavy-handed in the situation they believe should be resolved by the use of professional skill. It may be frustrating to leave the social workers at this point facing their dilemma, but it highlights the uncertainty they face and the fact that the subject-matter of the book is the processes of making sound decisions whose further exploration need to await the subsequent chapters.

Evaluating the decision making

At some point in the future the social workers or another party may come to evaluate the decision taken that afternoon. Decision

FIGURE 1.2 *A decision making framework for professional social work*

7. Evaluating

Have you considered whether:

the decision making was sound,

the decision implementation is proving viable and

the decision outcome achieved the decision goals.

⇧

6. Choosing an Option

For each option have you considered:

the possible outcomes in terms of what they are, their relative value and their likelihood and

whether there are any points of principle that need to be considered alongside or instead of considerations of outcomes and

what role emotions are playing in the choice.

⇧

5. Framing the Decision Situation

Have you and the stakeholders:

developed a holistic picture of the situation taking into account all relevant factors,

identified decision goals,

clearly identified a set of options and

considered potential distortions.

Decision Making

4. Thinking and Feeling about the Decision Situation

Have you and the stakeholders:

considered whether this decision requires analysis,

checked that inappropriate short cuts in your thinking are not being taken and

been aware of the emotions involved and the impact they are having.

⇦

1. Decision Making Contexts

Are you critically taking into account the decision making contexts including:

the aim of social work,
the nature of society,
the relevant legal requirements,
the relevant policy decisions,
the nature of the agency and the work of other agencies.

⇩

2. Involving the Client

Have you worked out with the client:

who the client/s are,

what level of involvement is being aimed for,

whether this is the highest level of involvement feasible and

how this level of involvement can be achieved.

⇩

3. Meeting with the Stakeholders

Have you considered with the client:

who the stakeholders are and who needs to meet together,

the issues of power between the stakeholders,

how the potential benefits of meeting together can be realised and

how any decisions within the meeting will be taken.

⇦

makers may be aware at the time that they are making a critical decision or this may only become clear sometime afterwards. If the social workers satisfactorily resolve the situation, it is likely that little further thought will be given to their decision. But if it is subsequently found that they failed to protect a child from further harm or they become the subject of a complaint about being heavy-handed, the decision could come under critical scrutiny. When the outcome is known a judgement can be made as to whether or not it was an effective decision that met their decision goals. The evaluation of decision making cannot always afford to wait for the outcome of the decision, which may be a considerable length of time in the future, so there needs to be a way of evaluating the decision making process before decision outcomes become known. Such an evaluation needs to be based on a clear understanding of what constitutes a sound decision, such as given by the framework presented in diagrammatic form in Figure 1.2. The subsequent chapters discuss in detail each of the seven elements of the framework, with the final chapter considering why bad outcomes can occur despite sound decision making.

CHAPTER SUMMARY AND KEY POINTS

Although decision making is a key part of social work, it has received comparatively little attention. This chapter has laid some of the ground before each aspect of the decision making framework is discussed in the following chapters. Decision making was defined as a process of making a choice, which in social work involves issues of taking into account the contexts, how to involve the client, consulting with the stakeholders, thinking and feeling clearly, framing complex decision situations, being clear about the basis of choice and evaluating these processes as well as the implementation and outcome of the decision.

When building a framework for decision making in social work, the following need to be considered:

- why decision making needs to become more of a specific focus within social work;
- what has prevented a clear focus on decision making in the past;
- what decision making in social work involves; and
- what sound decision making entails.

Issues and tensions when building a framework for decision making in social work include:

- the interconnections between the different aspects of decision making in social work – for example, involving the client and working with the stakeholders;
- the different perspectives on decision making in social work – for example, client, professional and managerial perspectives; and
- that decision making in social work needs to be understood on a number of different levels – for example, thinking, feeling, interpersonal, organisational and societal levels.

2

Decision Making Contexts

Decision makers need to be critically aware of, take into account and act upon the contexts in which the decision is being made. What is meant by context can be problematic, but here will be taken to refer to the requirements, structures and conditions surrounding the decision making, while the central focus of the client's social situation will be considered in Chapter 6 'Framing the Decision Situation'. In this chapter the societal context, the legal requirements, policy decisions, agency conditions and the work of other agencies will be discussed in relation to social work's endeavours to enhance human well-being. These contextual opportunities and constraints are generally beyond the immediate influence of individual social workers, who may be considered to have a moral obligation to join with others to bring about necessary changes.

ILLUSTRATIVE EXAMPLE

John is a 14-year-old young person who lives in a children's home known as The Grove. He is in the care of the local authority and has a history of self-harm and absconding. Leroy, John's key worker, is a residential social worker. The staff team are having a weekly meeting with John to discuss the previous week and plan for the next. John had cut himself last week in response to Leroy calling another member of staff, when John had come to his room wanting to talk at three o'clock in the morning. John's self-harm behaviour is raising a question mark over the suitability of The Grove to meet his needs. The discussion has centred around John's forthcoming child care review and the issue of his possible transfer to the authority's own therapeutically oriented secure unit. The local child psychiatrist, while giving support and consultation to The Grove staff, is not prepared to admit John to the child and adolescent unit without John's consent.

The Aim of Social Work

Decision making contexts need to be considered in relation to the aim of professional social work that can generally be characterised as 'the enhancement of human well being' (BASW, 1996). Leroy regarding himself as a professional social worker brings to the task of residential child care the broad aim of enhancing John's well-being with due regard to the well-being of others. There is likely to be a measure of agreement about this broad aim, while opinions may differ as to what human well-being actually entails, how it can best be achieved, and what priority is to be given to achieving it when there are competing claims. Endeavours to achieve this aim need to be set in the context of the difficult and contradictory tasks undertaken by social workers on behalf of society, which by their very nature can involve both the care and control of clients. Society may be more interested in social control and providing a service of last resort at minimum cost, than the enhancement of human well being (Bamford, 1990, p. 160). Having an aim should not be confused with its achievement and social work's success or failure in enhancing human well-being, both in general and in a particular case, needs to be judged in relation to the resources made available and the adverse circumstances in which clients typically live.

The contexts discussed in this chapter are both potential opportunities and potential constraints to the achievement of the general aim of social work. To have a chance of this being achieved, social workers will need to: (i) assert values that stress the well-being of the client; (ii) develop holistic understandings of social situations and (iii) formulate, act upon and evaluate effective plans that foster human well-being. These can be regarded as general principles of practice, the detailed meanings of which are, and need to remain, sites of contention. The decision making contexts discussed are potential sources of pressure to abandon these principles, with the result that there can be a large gap between ideals and what actually happens in practice. If social workers are to further their professional aim they need to be able to imaginatively find a way through the contextual constraints and develop the opportunities that do exist. Before considering the contexts of decision making, the three principles of practice will be outlined a little further.

Asserting certain values

Statements of social work values can be seen as guidelines about suitable approaches to practice that are developed over a period of time within a particular national boundary that indicate difficult areas of practice rather than certainties (Payne, 1996, chapter 4). What the values of social work are in detail and how they can best be formulated are contested areas (see Banks, 1995, chapter 3). This lack of agreement should not be allowed to mask the fact that, given the aim of professional social work, social workers involved in decision making need to assert values that stress the well-being of the client. In the context of structural inequalities, this will include 'attempts to confront or resist injustice or the abuse of power' (Thomas and Pierson, 1997, p. 19). Professional values need to come to the fore when there is a conflict about what to do, such as the uncertainty about John's future, but these can be in competition with other values – for example, economic, organisational or personal values. The Grove's management is presenting the sugges-tion that John be moved as being in his best interests, but Leroy fears that John is being sacrificed to ease the burden on the staff team. In Leroy's view the management team are placing more value on the smooth running of The Grove than on John's future well-being.

Understanding people in their social situations

Agency management can attempt to proceduralise and routinise assessment, but from a professional social work point of view each situation is unique and what may be required in one situation may not be appropriate in another, even quite similar, situation. Leroy believes there is an attempt to simplify John's situation, with his self-harm behaviour being equated with specialist care, whereas social situations are complex and not amenable to the routine and mechanical application of procedures. These matters need to be matters of judgement based on the particulars of the situation and values that stress the individuality of the client and their circum-stances. Leroy believes it is important to understand John's actions in context and what these indicate about his needs. This will entail

Leroy developing an understanding that takes into account a wide range of factors. He is endeavouring to develop such an understanding of John's self-harm behaviour which includes seeing it as his way of coping with his strong emotions in relation to feeling abandoned by his father.

Acting in ways that foster human well-being

As a matter of principle and a matter of effectiveness, clients and other stakeholders need to be engaged in carefully formulating, acting upon and evaluating plans constructed to promote human well-being. Leroy, as John's key worker, has included John, his mother, and a network of other professionals in constructing a carefully tailored plan, which involves the maintenance and fostering of contact with his mother, re-establishing regular school attendance and his preparation for independent living. The difficult situations within social work can provoke a reactive practice that militates against the sustained implementation of plans. Professional social work endeavours to be purposeful, whereas there can be pressure to 'manage' situations rather than work towards planned change. Leroy believes that the management team's response to John's absconding and self-harm are putting John's care plan in jeopardy and some members of staff are coming to believe that The Grove is no longer an appropriate placement for him. There will be pressure at the forthcoming review to abandon the carefully worked out plan in a reactive response to John's difficult behaviour.

The Nature of the Society

Decision makers need to be critically aware of the society in which the decision situation is located, yet its everyday familiarity can make this difficult. On one level the decision situation has been produced by that society and its complete resolution, and the prevention of similar problems developing in future, are dependent on changes in its structure, an approach that has been termed structural social work (Mullaly, 1993). Two dimensions of society will be considered: the social structure and the cultural climate. Each of these is a complex area of study in its own right and it is beyond the scope of this book to give more than a sketch of how they form a context for decision making in social work.

Social structure of society

Clients tend to be located at the bottom end of prevalent structures of inequality and oppression. Enhancing human well-being in such circumstances is, to say the least, very difficult. For example, the poverty John and his mother have lived in has had a profound effect on their lives and has made positive changes difficult for them to achieve. Life on a low income impacts on family life and 'can result in poor diet, lack of fuel and water, poor housing and homelessness, debt, poor physical health, and stress and mental health problems' (Kempson, 1996, p. 30). The estate they lived on was highly stigmatised, the levels of unemployment were very high, the housing stock in poor condition, and the general environment bleak, with high levels of crime, scanty community facilities and under-resourced schools. If John is to grow into a well-adjusted adult, he has many adverse circumstances to overcome and Leroy's endeavours to work with him need to be seen in this context of a lack of opportunity and a negative environment. Some approaches to social work emphasise the need to tackle the causes of social problems rather than just ameliorating their symptoms. This can be seen either as a rival approach to individual- and family-focused work or as its logical extension. While many social workers would agree with the analysis that the problems clients face have their root cause in the structure of society, they can also point to the lack of practical strategies emerging from this analysis.

John and his parents live in a society in which deep social changes are occurring in the ways people live their lives. John has also grown up at a time of changing institutional structures in society, including patterns of family life and gender roles, with 'thirty-seven per cent of first marriages end[ing] in divorce' (Gorell Barnes, 1991, p. 145). Members of society and social provisions can be ill prepared for such social changes and there can be 'gaps in parenting offered to children following family break-up' (Gorell Barnes, 1991, p. 145). It is as if there is a time-lag between social changes and the expectations, roles and actions of individuals. When John's parents separated a number of years ago, they were unable to continue to work together as parents and John was drawn into the antagonism between them. John responded by becoming very difficult. While his mother struggled to keep control of him she found herself isolated and under stress. John's father gradually lost contact with his son, while John increasingly resented his mother's new partner and now dreams of one day finding his father and going to live with him. Leroy cannot undo the social changes that were part and parcel of John's parents' break-up; rather, he sees himself helping John find better ways of coping with his strong emotions and finding a path forward in his life.

Cultural climate

Changes in the cultural climate may create periods of heightened sensitivity that can have an undue influence on the focus of concern. Prevailing values and beliefs about what is a problem, what causes it or who is to blame and how it can be overcome form an important backdrop to decision making in social work. One characteristic of society is that from time to time it can be beset by a moral panic over a particular social issue. At such times, decision makers need to consider whether they are being unduly influenced by the current moral panic or fashion. In the midst of a professional or public unease it may be difficult to distinguish between a mis-informed moral panic and the development of awareness of a legitimate cause for concern. For example, in a series of steps during the latter part of the twentieth century, the different ways children can be abused were increasingly recognised, with a progressive understanding that children can be harmed – physically, sexually and emotionally – within differing contexts by individuals and organised groups. Points of discovery can be accompanied by a heightened sensitivity, which has some of the features of a moral panic, during which there can be problems in distinguishing between a considered response and overreaction.

Many physically abused children were detected during the 1970s but at times indiscriminate searches for bruises also led to some injustices. This was superseded by the discovery of sexual abuse within families during the 1980s and the discovery in the 1990s of sexual abuse of children in care by paedophiles who had infiltrated the care system. Each of these represents a development of the awareness and acknowledgement of the abuse of children in society, but in the periods of discovery there can be a temporary over-reaction. The latest incident of John cutting himself was triggered when Leroy followed the procedure and called another member of staff so as not to be alone with John at night. The procedures were designed to protect both staff and residents, drawn up in the context of concerns about young people being sexually abused by staff. Nevertheless, John's simple request for support became a major hazard for Leroy, amidst the national concerns about the abuse of children by residential staff. As Minty (1995, p.50) argues, scandals can produce an automatic management response of tightening procedures with the consequent danger of a potential loss of sensitivity.

The mass media can play an important role in reflecting and developing social concerns and at times can produce a hostile climate in which decisions are made. The local press have been running a series of stories about the 'goings on' at The Grove. The mass media portrayal of social workers shows an ambivalent and contradictory attitude towards social work, reflected in the request, 'clean up the dirt but don't do it by damaging people like us'. Social workers are accused of being both too zealous and not zealous enough, or in the words of Franklin and Parton (1991, p. 16), being fools or wimps, or villains and bullies. When social workers and their agencies feel under attack from the mass media and the general public, they can become defensive in their work, producing an excessive concern with safety and a corresponding unwillingness to take risks. Leroy believes his line manager is currently being overly defensive in the management of John's situation for fear of criticism in the light of a recent suicide of a young person in care which received extensive negative coverage in the local press.

The Relevant Legal Requirements

The law is an important context in making a decision since it gives agencies and workers powers and duties, and citizens rights and safeguards. The general law forms a background but there are also specific laws that can provide a framework for making particular decisions. Some decisions will have a strong legal dimension, whereas others may not have specific legal requirements. Decisions concerning a person's liberty are understandably highly regulated by the law, but other decisions like deciding whether the time has come for the work with a client to come to an end are relatively unregulated. An important issue is how to achieve an appropriate balance, one which recognises the important role law plays in social work and not letting this develop into an overemphasis on legal matters to the exclusion of others.

Legalistic or holistic approach?

There is no shortage of texts setting out the legal context in detail (for example, see Vernon, 1990; Mallinson, 1992; and Mandelstam, 1995). The exact position of law in relation to social work can be disputed between it being *the* central determining focus and being *one* of a number of important considerations (Braye and Preston Shoot, 1992, p. 2). It is not contested that knowledge of the law is essential for social workers but that such knowledge in isolation should not determine decisions alone. The law can provide a framework for what the options are, but a solely legalistic view is too narrow to accommodate all the diversity and complexity of decision situations in social work. As Olive Stevenson states:

> The image of the social worker as 'agent of the law' is . . . partial and dangerous. For it encourages a view of professional compe-tence which rests solely or mainly on an ability to interpret and execute legal requirements, whereas, in fact, such competence rests on far wider abilities in which that elusive but crucial element of professional judgement is central. (Stevenson, 1986, p. 503)

There will not always be a conflict between a legalistic perspective and a more holistic one. Much law is based on principles of good practice and can give a specific duty to social workers to safeguard a client's well-being. Nevertheless the law, by its very nature, can only give the basic requirements; in a specific case, this can fall short of what is needed. For example, the Children Act 1989 gives young people the right to be consulted about decisions, which is an important but limited right, that in many situations will not be the highest feasible level of involvement (see Chapter 3). In the example, John is being listened to, with his wishes and feelings being taken into account, but the agency management and professional staff can still decide what they consider to be in his best interests.

Knowledge and understanding of the relevant statutes and regulations and the availability of legal advice are needed if social workers are to be critically aware of the legal requirements. In the deliberations about John's future placement, a clear understanding of the legal provisions and safeguards concerning the restriction of his liberty is necessary. For example, the staff at The Grove are aware that the care of John comes under the Children Act 1989 and the option of restricting John's liberty would need to be considered in relation to section 25 of that Act. This sets out the criteria which would need to apply, the most relevant part to John's situation being 'that if he is kept in any other description of accommodation [other than secure accommodation] he is likely to injure himself . . .'. Many young people may fall within the criteria whose circumstances, from a professional point of view, would not justify the restriction of their liberty. The discussion at The Grove has tended to revolve around whether a convincing legal argument could be put forward to allow the court to authorise the restriction of John's liberty. Leroy believes that professionally the question is much wider. He feels that rejecting John is the worst thing they could do and that they need to stick with him during this difficult period in his life. Leroy believes that the legislation provides an important framework within which decisions can be taken, but that it should not be allowed to determine decisions in a narrow way.

Knowledge of the law necessary but not sufficient

Even when laws are designed to safeguard clients' rights, they will not do so in the absence of good practice on the part of a number of stakeholders. Laws may ostensibly safeguard and protect people, but they can also be used to control them, often with the stated objective of protecting them from themselves. Section 25 of the Children Act 1989 empowers the Secretary of State to make regulations that specify a maximum period beyond which a child may not be kept in secure accommodation without the authority of the court. The regulations known as the *Children (Secure Accommodation) Regulations 1991* give the period as 72 hours within any 28-day period. The implications of having to seek authorisation of a court under the Children Act 1989 is that the child's welfare is the court's paramount consideration and an order will not be made unless the court considers that doing so would be better for the child than making no order at all. There is also provision for the child to be legally represented and the appointment of a guardian *ad litem*. These are examples of the safeguards provided by legislation, but the courts have often been found to 'rubber stamp' the applications of agencies and professionals, with 'a combination of weak case, strong solicitor and independent-minded court . . . [being] necessary for an application to fail' (Harris and Timms, 1993, p. 140). There is usually the potential for a positive use of the law, but good professional practice is needed on the part of a number of stake-holders, including social workers, before this potential can be realised. Although statutes and regulations often promote what would be professionally regarded as good practice and 'can be used to benefit and empower' clients (Dalrymple and Burke, 1995, p. 23) they only do so in the context of good professional practice.

The Relevant Policy Decisions

What is meant by the term policy is by no means straightforward or agreed (Hill, 1997, p. 6). In the discussion that follows, the term will be used in a restricted sense to denote the existence of a set of previous decisions or stance about what actions are to be followed in particular types of situation. The existence of policy in this sense can lessen the role of professional discretion and judgement, but having a policy can bring consistency to decision making and enable the policy makers' aims to be achieved. Rarely are policies sufficiently detailed to dictate what to do in a particular situation and for them to do so is neither feasible nor desirable. What impact policy has on social workers' attempts to enhance the human well-being of clients has to remain an open question depending on the content and nature of the policy in question. Policies rarely remove the need to make a decision but rather set the parameters in which decisions are made. Decision making in a particular situation can involve deciding whether a policy applies, whether to follow the policy, how to interpret the policy or whether a particular case is an exception to the policy or not.

Government policy

A government's social and economic policy impacts on the lives of clients and the work of social workers and so contributes to the shape of the general environment in which decisions are made. Government policy can also have a specific impact as in the example of giving agencies and social workers written practice guidance with the expectation that this will be followed. Johnson

(1972, p.77) gives the state control of social services in the UK as an example of mediative control, as opposed to self-control or consumer control of a profession. In seeking to influence or control what social workers do, the UK government has issued volumes of official guidance in the areas of child care and community care (Payne, 1997a). Payne argues that the guidance is authoritative in character, uses primarily official sources, is authored by government employees, focused on professional decision making and practice and reinforces the government's partial views of the role of social work (Payne, 1997a). Although the precise legal standing of such guidance remains unclear (Allen, 1992, p. 9), the child care guidance is issued under Section 7 of the Local Authority Social Services Act 1997 and so 'has considerable force in almost requiring compliance with it' (Payne, 1997a, p. 383).

In terms of presenting a constraint or opportunity to furthering the professional aim of social work of enhancing human welfare, it is hardly surprising that government publications tend to be one dimensional. Nevertheless their content is Janus faced, at times adding strength to professional arguments. For example, the *Children Act 1989: Guidance and Regulations: Volume 4 Residential Care* states that:

> restricting the liberty of children is a serious step which must be taken only when there is no appropriate alternative. It must be a 'last resort' in the sense that all else must first have been comprehensively considered and rejected – never because no other placement was available at the relevant time, [or] because of inadequate staffing. (Department of Health, 1991b, p. 118)

Whereas in work with adults, the *Practitioners' Guide to Care Management and Assessment* effectively leaves the determination of need to agency policy by defining need as:

> the requirements of individuals to enable them to achieve, maintain or restore an acceptable level of social independence or quality of life, as defined by the particular care agency or authority. (Social Services Inspectorate/Social Work Services Group, 1991, p. 12)

The danger of leaving it to agencies to define need is that assessment can become an administrative technical task involving the filling in of forms with the purpose of rationing resources, rather than a professional one of complex analysis with the purpose of enhancing human well-being. A *critical* awareness rather than a mechanical application of government guidance is needed, to promote an opening-up rather than a narrowing of possibilities in decision making. Government guidance can be seen as promoting good professional practice, but it is also a means of controlling what social workers do. Payne argues that the sometimes enthusiastic acceptance on the part of social workers of this guidance indicates 'a pact between government and social workers in the UK' under which the government can implement its policy objectives by giving guidance and workers can protect themselves from criticism by following government advice (Payne, 1997a, p. 388).

Agency policy

Even though governments may strongly influence or even determine what agencies do, there is always considerable scope for agencies to formulate their own policies within the context of laws, regulations and guidance from government departments. The agency's policies may be set out in general statements or reflected in detailed procedures. A distinction sometimes needs to be made between formal agency policy and actual organisational practice. In Leroy's agency it is policy for the principal officer (child care) to make the decision whether to apply to a court for authorisation to restrict a young person's liberty. This is the formal level of decision making but there can be a difference between this and the effective level of decision making when decisions are merely 'rubber stamped' at the formal level (Harris and Timms, 1993, p. 88). The impact of such a policy will depend on whether the principal officer (child care) takes a gatekeeping approach of saying 'no' for as long as he or she can or adopts a professional concern and responsibility to develop alternatives in what is a very difficult situation.

Agency policy may have more to do with rationing resources than the enhancement of human well-being. The availability of resources is perhaps one of the most important contextual factors constraining decision making. In order to gatekeep an expensive resource, agencies tend to develop policy in terms of restrictive criteria. For example, an authority may have their own criteria for secure accommodation that is tighter than the one contained in the Children Act 1989 (Harris and Timms, 1993, pp. 90–1). In this particular instance professional social work may welcome an agency's tight restrictive criteria since it is likely to restrict the inappropriate use of secure accommodation. However, an inflexible policy may not allow secure accommodation authorisation to be applied for when it is genuinely in the interests of the young person. Resources do need to be rationed but the balance achieved between financial considerations and the needs of clients will impact on whether agency policy is a constraint or an opportunity to enhance human well-being. One of the crucial issues for social workers is whether they would rather ration the resources themselves or be able to blame agency management for doing so. Up until now 'British social work has sought to distance itself from money' (Lewis, Bernstock, Bovell and Wookey, 1996, p. 9), something that is becoming increasingly difficult with the introduction of those care management approaches that involve the so-called micro, as opposed to the macro, purchasing of services and which entail front-line social workers being involved in balancing budgets.

The Nature of the Agency

Leroy is an employee of a large social services department, but the size and the nature of social work organisations can vary considerably. When an agency consists of more than one setting it may be necessary to consider agency and setting separately and the interaction between the two. Social workers can be characterised as professional workers located in bureaucratic organisations and have been referred to as 'bureau-professionals' (Parry *et al.*, 1979, p. 43). From social work's earliest history there has been a recognition of a tension between achieving the aim of social work and agency function. From a professional perspective social workers are not mere functionaries of agencies but members of a profession who are employed by agencies, who as front-line workers retain considerable discretion (see Lipsky, 1997). The degree of autonomy is conditional on agencies being dependent on social workers' skills in assessing and responding to unique and uncertain decision situations – a task not amenable to the application of rigid rules. Although there may be an inherent tension between social workers and agency managers, the structure and culture of an agency can either support or undermine professional social work practice.

Organisational structure: social workers and managers

Despite the diversity of operational structures of agencies (Challis, 1990), a typical agency management structure is hierarchical, with a number of layers each accountable to the one above. There can be successive layers of management above social workers, with a distinction needing to be made between the upper management of the agency and the setting management. The degree of difficulty agency conditions present professional social work depends on the extent agency managers endeavour to control what social workers do and the extent to which social workers are content to be controlled. One issue is whether agency managers are *social work* managers whose values are rooted in social work or *general* professional managers with values rooted in managerialism. Another issue is whether the agency management's attitude towards professional social work is sympathetic or hostile. Related to these two factors is the extent to which agency managers engage in de-professionalising social work tasks and so control more of what social workers do. Such control might be achieved by the imposition of routines, rules and procedures and the requirement that anything falling outside these be referred up the management structure for a decision. Under the influence of managerialism, managers have gained more power to control social workers in the drive for efficiency, standardisation and the targeting of resources and pressure to implement new legislation (Pahl, 1994).

The other side of the equation is the extent to which social workers accept management control or are in a position to resist it. In the face of demands, social workers can hide behind the need for those higher up the hierarchy to make decisions. An ambivalent attitude towards the hierarchical structure can be displayed with it being both their 'protective stronghold' in relation to external demands and the 'bane of their lives' internally within the agency, as when the social workers in Woodhouse and Pengelly's study:

> faced outwards towards other agencies, the courts and the demanding public it was this very monolithic quality that became their protective stronghold. The hierarchical organisation (internally the bane of their lives) enabled them to shelter behind decisions made at a higher level, or to put off urgent demands by explaining that they would have to refer upwards for such decisions to be made. (Woodhouse and Pengelly, 1991, p. 86)

Leroy could distance himself from the decision about John's future, maintaining it was one to be taken by management, or he could see himself having an important role in endeavouring to influence it. Which course he follows may depend on the extent to which he has passively accepted his place both in the hierarchy and the division of labour of the agency.

Supervision has had an important place within professional social work, being the arena in which setting managers meet with social workers. However, there is a distinction between professional supervision and managerial supervision (see Payne, 1994, pp. 43–58). Professional supervision helps social workers contain the contradictory demands, complexity and uncertainty of professional social work, while managerial supervision emphasises control of the worker by checking whether agency procedures have been followed. Traditionally, supervision has been seen as a blend of both elements in balance with each other, providing a forum for the sounding-out of ideas and understandings and the provision of support, information, and the authority of the agency. In terms of the agency conditions for professional social work, the questions are whether reasonable quality of supervision is available and whether the managerial element has come to dominate.

Agency culture

The culture of an organisation is complex and multi-layered and relates to values and routines. It features custom and practice, established routines, expectations and dominant attitudes. Another way of looking at the relationship between managers and social workers is whether a particular agency has a 'professional' or 'procedural' culture and whether the agency culture supports creativity and risk taking in decision making or promotes defensiveness and fear. Thompson draws the distinction between a 'culture of commitment' in which staff share the goals of management and a 'culture of compliance' in which they do not (Thompson *et al.*, 1996, p. 649). Agencies can also have what Thompson refers to as a negative culture (Thompson *et al.*, 1996, p. 650) in which the organisation becomes dysfunctional. In the chapter study, Leroy's agency could be characterised as having a culture of compliance, where many of the staff experience alienation and feel the need to protect themselves by mechanically following the procedures. This impacts on, but does not determine, the distinctive culture of The Grove.

Setting culture

The Grove's culture can be seen as consisting of different interlocking groups: the group of young people, the staff group and the setting management group. Each of these can have a distinctive culture of their own. Settings like agencies can have a formal and an informal culture that exist alongside each other. The informal culture can have more impact on day-to-day work and may be in conflict with the formal culture. The Grove can be identified as a *participative* culture where the setting management, professional staff and residents endeavour to work together and support each other – an example of which is John being involved in the weekly staff discussions concerning his care. This contrasts with an *autocratic* culture in which management gives directives to staff, who in turn give them to residents. The culture of a setting is related to many factors, including whether the relationship between the different groups is co-operative or antagonistic, whether a common philosophy has been established and whether leadership is provided. Enhancing human well-being will be more difficult in a setting whose culture runs counter to the aims of professional social work.

Delineation of tasks and roles

There are differing views as to how professional social work is best organised (for example, see La Valle and Lyons, 1996, p. 8). One view is that the key to professional social work is holism with social work at its core being a generic activity concerned with people, families and communities as a whole, with a process that has a coherence of its own that is destroyed by division. This view can be complemented by believing that good practice depends on the development of specialist knowledge and skills on the part of some workers, particularly those located in specialist settings, while the core of professional social work remains generalist. A counter view is that social work needs to be divided into specific tasks and roles in relation to particular groups, if social workers and their agencies are not to be swamped by uncontrollable demand and lack of clear purpose and priorities. There is not necessarily a contradiction between the need to recognise the general core skills of social work and the need for specialist social workers. Voluntary agencies which have been set up to work with particular types of problem or particular groups of people require social workers with specialist skills. Even when an agency's function is quite wide, its work is often organised in a way that both depends on specialising with particular groups and having a division of labour between the different aspects of the process of social work, particularly assessment and implementation. The problem is that where this takes an extreme form it simplifies and standardises tasks and so reduces the ability of social workers to respond holistically to an individual's unique needs.

Leroy's agency is organised into child care services and adult services, a division which has benefits as well as drawbacks. For example, John's mother has mental health difficulties and is a client of the mental health team. This division of responsibilities has enabled both sets of workers to develop specialist skills and knowledge in their respective areas. Nevertheless, despite efforts to work closely together it has also had the consequence of the family and its members not being seen as a whole and the work with them becoming fragmented. Child care services are further divided, into providers and care management. Leroy and The Grove are located in the providers' division and even though the split is not so well developed as in adult services (see Lewis, Bernstock, Bovell and Wookey, 1996), one negative aspect has been the further institutionalisation of the separation of assessment of need from the day-to-day provision of care. This has exacerbated the tension that had always existed between field social workers and residential social workers in child care. Leroy feels he will have a limited influence on the decision about whether John is moved from The Grove. As John's key worker, Leroy believes he has an important contribution to make to the continuing assessment of John's needs, but the way the agency is organised is undermining this by endeavouring to separate assessment decisions from service provision.

The Work of Other Agencies

The last context of social work decision making to be considered is the work of other agencies. Working with and seeking to influence other agencies for the benefit of the client is part of social work. A number of agencies are involved with John's situation, including the child and adolescent mental health service, the police, the education department and the local secondary school. In both child care and adult care services, much emphasis is placed on inter-agency and inter-professional working with social workers working alongside the workers of other agencies (for example, see Øvretveit, 1993; Hallett, 1995), but whether this co-operation is always directed at enhancing the well-being of the client is open to question. This can hinge around how the boundaries between the agencies are maintained and the nature of the dynamics between them.

Maintaining agency boundaries

Given the nature of the decision situations that social service agencies deal with, there is a tendency for other agencies to be simultaneously involved with the client or to have a potential role. Each agency has its own function and endeavours to maintain a boundary around its work. Decision makers need to be aware of which other agencies are involved (or need to be involved) in the decision situation, their role and potential contribution, so that co-operation and co-ordination can be fostered. Points of tension can arise, often stemming from the desire of each agency to protect its boundary.

Disputes can occur over whose responsibility a client is or whose job it is to carry out a particular task. This can take the form of a perceived encroachment into another agency's role, seeing the other agencies as reneging on their responsibilities or making strenuous efforts to keep the agency boundary tight so as not to be swamped by external demands. The staff of The Grove feel that the child and adolescent mental health service have a direct responsibility for 'disturbed' young people like John, which cannot be met by providing consultation alone. These kinds of tensions are more likely when there is an overlap of skills, confusion about roles or differences in philosophy. There is a need for each agency to appreciate the distinctive roles and boundaries of other agencies while allowing for co-operation, but often there are emotions involved that may have little to do with agency function. Woodhouse and Pengelly found that maintaining the agency boundary was one way of defending against anxiety, when social workers managed 'the fear of being swamped with human problems for which there was no solution . . .[by having] a dour persistence and painstaking thoroughness within the limits of the narrowly defined task' (Woodhouse and Pengelly, 1992, p. 185).

Inter-agency dynamics

Difficult decision situations can evoke anxiety with a tendency to draw in as many other agencies as possible or search for a particular agency to offload uncertainty onto. There will be a history of relations between two agencies – for example, the staff of both agencies may feel unappreciated by the other. In the case study, there has been a history of suspicion, mistrust and some hostility between Leroy's agency and the local child and adolescent mental health service. The social services department have tended to see the adolescent mental health service as unhelpful and too choosy about the situations they get involved in, while they in turn have tended to perceive the social services department as trying to indiscriminately offload its difficult young people onto them. Decision makers need to be aware of these dynamics and endeavour not to let them interfere with decision making. One agency can be seen as negatively impacting on the work of another and may become a scapegoat onto which negative emotions can be deposited. For example, the decision by John's school to exclude him has had a profound impact on the work of The Grove staff team. John is now around the home all day, and only receives three hours of personal tuition a week, provided by the education department. The Grove staff believe the school should have been more tolerant of John's behaviour, while the school staff feel the social services department do not fully appreciate that they have to be concerned about the education of *all* their pupils, not just John.

CHAPTER SUMMARY AND KEY POINTS

This chapter has argued that social workers need to be critically aware of the contexts in which decisions are made, which present both opportunities and constraints for promoting human well-being. These contexts may be outside the immediate and direct influence of the individual social worker, but part of the wider professional task is joining with others to bring about necessary changes to resolve the present decision situation and prevent similar problems developing in future.

When taking into account the contexts in which decisions are being made, the following need to be considered:

- the aim of social work;
- the nature of the society;
- the relevant legal requirements;
- the relevant policy decisions;
- the nature of the agency; and
- the work of other agencies.

Issues and tensions when taking into account decision making contexts include:

- the contradictory demands placed on social workers by society and the less than ideal contexts in which decisions are often made;
- not allowing any one particular context to have a mechanical determining influence; and
- building on the opportunities within the contexts while not being undermined by the constraints.

3

Involving the Client

In various guises a core value of social work has been that clients should have direct involvement in decision making (see Payne, 1989), but this has not always been put into practice. Within a decision making framework, the focus is on decisions that concern the client's own life situation and the services she or he receives, but clients may also need to be collectively involved in deciding agency policy and the general service provision (Beresford and Croft, 1993; Forbes and Sashidharan, 1997). Three issues of client involvement are discussed in this chapter: firstly, identifying the client is not always straightforward and in many decision situations there is more than one client; secondly, there are different levels of involvement and in some decision situations there may be a ceiling on the highest achievable level; and thirdly, active steps may be needed so that the client feels sufficiently empowered to become involved.

ILLUSTRATIVE EXAMPLE

Ann is a 37-year-old single parent caring for her two daughters, aged 15 and 13. Four months ago Ann had refused drug treatment for her anxiety and depression and her GP referred her to the community mental health team. Sandra, a social work member of the team, has been working with Ann in relation to her low self-esteem. The time has come to review the care plan, which Ann wants to continue as she feels a need for support and encouragement, but Sandra's team manager wants the case closed because she has a higher-priority case she wishes to allocate urgently to Sandra. Sandra is having doubts about the work continuing in its present form, believing it is in danger of becoming counter-productive, with Ann relying on her too much for emotional support. Nevertheless, she believes the work needs to continue in a re-focused form or the gains that have been made will be lost.

Who is the Client?

It is not uncommon for there to be more than one client in a decision situation and careful consideration needs to be given as to who the clients are. Within the way the community mental health team and Sandra have framed their work, Ann is the sole client, but there are a number of other ways the situation could have been considered. The family group, possibly including Ann's two daughters and her boyfriend, could be regarded as the client either as a household or wider network (see O'Sullivan, 1994). Another view would be to work with Ann and her 15-year-old daughter, who has taken on a caring role. When there is more than one client, it may be necessary to make a distinction between *primary clients* and *secondary clients*.

Primary and secondary clients

The primary client or clients will be defined as the person or persons whose welfare is the central focus. The secondary client or clients will be defined as the person or persons whose welfare is an important but indirect focus. The welfare of primary and secondary clients are usually inextricably bound up with each other and being a primary or secondary client does not necessarily reflect decision making responsibility or who the face-to-face work is with, but the prime purpose of the work. If Sandra was working in a child care team, the children would be the primary clients and Ann the secondary client. The focus would be the welfare of the children but Ann, being their parent, would be an important party. The children's welfare is bound up with their mother's welfare and unless there were good reasons to the contrary she would have the responsibility for making decisions in respect of them.

A similar situation can occur in adult services. There is usually a clearly identifiable person who can be considered the primary client in the sense that he or she is the person seeking assistance or has an impairment of some kind or is disabled in some way. But there are often other people centrally involved in a caring role, whose well-being has a direct impact on the welfare of the client. Though potentially they can have contradictory needs, their future well-being is often bound up with each other. The carer's welfare is affected by their caring role and the welfare of the primary client very much depends on the welfare of the carer who has needs of his or her own, something recognised by the Carers (Recognition and Services) Act 1995. When the carer is a child, particular considera- tion will need to be given to her or his needs (Aldridge and Becker, 1993).

When there is more than one client

Promoting involvement in decision making is more complex in situations which are considered to have more than one client, whether they are all considered primary clients or some of them considered secondary clients. Negotiations can be difficult and agreements harder to reach since there are more people to include. There needs to be recognition that there are different parties involved and there may not be agreement between them as to what course of action should be taken. When the focus of work is a family group, community group or network, important differences between group members will usually exist, with group member power and group dynamics entering the picture. These issues are dealt with in more detail in the next chapter when the stakeholders meeting together is discussed.

What Level of Involvement?

The second problematic area is the different levels of involvement clients can have and the way the nature of a decision can place a limit on the amount of involvement considered appropriate. In the late 1960s Arnstein put forward her influential eight-rung ladder of citizen participation (Arnstein, 1969). In the discussion below, four levels of client involvement will be identified: being told, being consulted, being a partner and being in control. Levels of involve- ment relate to specific decisions, not to clients, so there can be different levels of involvement when there are a number of decisions to be made in a particular situation. When considering the level of involvement, it is important to be clear about why the next level of involvement is not considered feasible.

Being told

The lowest level of involvement is *being told* the result of decision making; this raises the issue as to why the client is not being consulted. In most decision situations consultation is feasible, but for consultation to be authentic, the person being consulted needs to have a potential influence on the decision. *Being told* is more honest than a sham consultation when social workers find themselves in situations in which the decision has already been taken by management or consultation would endanger others. The belief that a decision is in the best interests of the client is no justification for *being told* as even a paternalistic approach allows for consultation. *Being told* represents no involvement at all, but even at this level there are still important issues of good practice, including whether the client is given a full, clear and understandable explanation as to why she was not consulted and informed of any means of redress available.

It may be difficult to think how the level of involvement in the example could be one of *being told*. The team manager and Sandra have in fact agreed that the decision should be taken at the review, but for a while Sandra was worried that despite her protests the team manager would direct her to terminate her work with Ann immediately and take on the new case. A number of thoughts went through Sandra's mind when she wondered what she would do if this happens. She considered resigning, but decided she could not afford to do so. She considered taking out a formal grievance, but believed it would get nowhere in an agency dominated by what is considered high-priority work, leaving little room for preventative work. Sandra came to the conclusion that she would have no choice but to tell Ann their work had to come to an end. She imagines explaining to Ann how it was a management decision that in the end she was unable to influence. In her mind's eye she sees Ann getting angry with her, threatening to turn her own case into a high-priority one, but fortunately none of this happens and the decision awaits the review.

Being consulted

The second level of involvement is that of *being consulted*, where the clients' opinions are taken into account when deciding what to do, a process familiar in the context of one professional consulting another (Brown, 1984) and managers consulting staff about changes. Consultation is a relatively low level of involvement with decisions being taken by the social worker or the agency and as a general principle all clients should at the very least be consulted about decisions that affect their lives and the services they receive. This includes people who may be considered not to have decision making capacity – for example, younger children, adults with severe dementia or a severe learning difficulty or who are regarded as severely mentally ill. This is feasible because consultation takes into account but does not necessarily act upon the opinion of the client.

Paternalism is when, despite consultation, the client's expressed wishes are opposed on the grounds that the social worker or agency knows better than the client what is in his or her best interests. Social workers always need both legal and moral authority to act in this paternalistic manner. Where there is no such authority, the implementation of decisions without the explicit consent of the client is unethical and maybe illegal. Consultation can easily be a sham, with the motions gone through but the client not being listened to, or what they say not being genuinely taken into account. The amount of influence clients have may depend on how much value is placed on fulfilling their wishes and the degree of under-standing they are regarded as having about their situation.

At the consultation level, it needs to be asked why the client is not a partner in decision making. There are a number of potential reasons why partnership may not be feasible. The agency may not seek the client's agreement when it is considered a decision for the agency to make with the client only being consulted. In other situations the agency may endeavour to make the decision in partnership but, despite the social workers' best efforts, agreement may not be reached, leaving the agency still needing to make a decision. Unless Ann is simply going to turn up to the review to be told the work is terminated, her level of involvement (on the face of it) is going to be, at the very least, consultation. This means Ann's reasons for wanting the work to continue will be listened to and taken into account.

Being a partner

The third level of involvement is *being a partner* when decisions are jointly made by the parties with agreement having being reached. Partnership is not always defined in this tight, and in some ways, restricted way (for example, see Marsh and Fisher, 1992) but one criticism has been that looser notions of partnership enable workers to feel better about their work, but do not benefit clients. If the case example decision was to be made on a partnership basis, Sandra, her team manager and Ann may jointly agree to continue or discontinue the work. When the parties have different starting positions, negotiation becomes a key process which involves recognising the right of each party to his or her own position and making concerted efforts to reach agreement. If all reasonable efforts to reach agreement fail, a move up or down the levels of involvement may become necessary. There is evidence that, when there is mediated negotiation between parties whose interests may substantially differ, agreements can be reached and kept over a period of time (Etter, 1993).

The notion of agreement is problematic, with it being questioned whether clients and social workers can be meaningfully referred to as reaching agreement in the context of social workers having 'a great deal more power than clients' (Rojek and Collins, 1987, p. 203). At the very least it needs to be recognised that there are different degrees of agreement, including resignation, acquiescence, acceptance, consent, consensus or enthusiasm. What form agreement takes will depend on the amount of concession or compromise involved and the extent to which a new viewpoint has developed. Furthermore, the degree to which participation is voluntary and agreement is freely given will determine whether it is partnership or coercion. Recording agreement in writing can bring greater clarity as to what has been agreed (Aldgate, 1989), but clients need to have been involved in deciding what goes into the written agreement, not feel obligated to sign and be fully aware of what they are agreeing to. Written agreements can work against partnership when they are used to maintain agency control (Dalrymple and Burke, 1995, p. 68) and when clients feel under pressure to sign despite reservations. Allowing external pressure to force an agreement is not only bad practice but counter-productive, since the nature of the agreement reached will impact on the degree of commitment to the agreed decision.

The team manager, Sandra and Ann will endeavour to negotiate with each other in order to reach agreement, but each is looking for a different decision. The team manager wants the case closed, Sandra wants the work re-focused with an agreed time-limit and Ann wants the work to continue in the same open-ended way, focusing on support. The question at this level of involvement is why can't the client be in control? There is a tendency for clients to

be considered as having control over some decisions and .
(Cupitt, 1997). Ann's right to refuse drug treatment h๛
respected and supported by Sandra and so, over this dec๋.
Ann can be regarded as having control. Her 15-year-old daughเ
wants her mother to go back to keeping a well-kept household,
whereas Ann has come to the opinion that housework is not
important. Sandra believes that in matters of lifestyle, clients should
be in control unless they are damaging themselves or other people.
The principle of self-determination gives clients control over their
own bodies and their own ways of life, as long as they are not
harming other people or, in some circumstances, themselves. This
principle of client control is not usually extended to deciding what
the level of service will be. Sandra's agency is unable or unwilling to
give Ann control over the level of service, as it believes it needs to
distribute scarce resources between competing claims and target
resources on those most in need.

Being in control

The highest level of involvement is *being in control*, when clients
take decisions for themselves with or without the facilitation of the
social worker. The client being in control can be considered the aim
of decision making in social work and there are many decision
situations where this can be achieved. When this is the level of
involvement the social worker needs to be clear as to who the
control is actually falling upon, as it may not be the client but
particular family or community members, as in family group
conferences (Lupton, 1998). There are situations when the client
being in control may not be feasible – for example, when they are a
danger to another person, or desirable – for example, when control
is inappropriately thrust on people who are not ready. There can
also be disingenuous attempts to empower people, for example,
when a decision situation is not allocated to a social worker
ostensibly to allow the person to make decisions for themselves,
when the real reason is to save on resources.

If it is accepted that resources need to be rationed so services can
be sustained, there are some substantial problems with Ann having
sole control over the decision. Ann is not in a position to balance
the competing claims on resources. If Ann is allowed to decide, the
higher-priority case could remain unallocated, leaving a potentially
dangerous person unsupervised in the community. This does not

mean that the agency cannot endeavour to make the decision in partnership with Ann. The agency could also formulate policy about priorities and how they are to be decided in consultation with a client action group. Nevertheless the determination of need, particularly the relative level of need, poses particular problems for agencies committed to client control in a context of limited resources.

Limits on the Level of Involvement

The orientation of social workers needs to be one of promoting the highest level of involvement feasible in the circumstances, with the assumption that clients have control over their own lives unless there are specific justifiable reasons why this should not be the case. So rather than considering what allows for the higher levels of involvement, the focus needs to be what prevents high involvement. The barriers to client involvement fall into two categories: those that can be regarded as necessary but problematic limits on the client's involvement and those that can be regarded as limiting factors that could and should be removed. Legitimate limits on the client's involvement could include: clients being a danger to themselves or to others, the age and understanding of children, a client's lack of decision making capacity and the need to fairly distribute limited resources. Other barriers can be regarded as unnecessary impediments that the social worker and client can work towards removing (see Braye and Preston-Shoot, 1995, p. 109).

Being a danger to self or others

There are times when it may be appropriate for clients *not* to determine courses of action because they are thought to be either a danger to themselves or to others. The issues of protecting clients from themselves may need to be distinguished from preventing clients from harming others. The former concerns whether paternalism, in the form of going against the expressed wishes of the client for his or her own good, can be justified (Gert and Culver, 1979). A common dilemma for social workers is whether clients should have autonomy to live their lives as they wish, no matter what dangers they put themselves in or whether to make paternalistic interventions to protect them from themselves (Abramson, 1985). The key issue in preventing the client from harming others is the reliability of the assessment that the client is a threat to the well-being of others. There will always be a degree of uncertainty as to whether the fears will materialise and it has become increasingly popular to think in terms of assessing the likelihood of them happening by means of a risk assessment (Campbell, 1995; Kemshall and Pritchard, 1996). Whether these provide a sound basis for making predictions of this nature is open to question (Wald and Woolverton, 1990), an issue that will be discussed further in Chapter 7. Ironically Ann could easily find herself in a reversal of her present situation, if she was considered to be at risk of harming herself or others and refused a service that she was thought to need. For example, if it was believed that there was a danger of Ann harming her daughters, she may be forced to receive a service in the form of compulsory detention in hospital under the Mental Health Act 1983.

Age and understanding of children

The level of involvement of children in decision making may vary as to their age and what is regarded as their level of understanding. The *being consulted* level is a matter of good practice and will often be a legal requirement (Department of Health, 1990, p. 12). The term Gillick competent has come into use after a court decision asserting that it was lawful for doctors to give contraceptive advice to a girl under 16 without the consent of her parents (Brandon, Schofield and Trinder, 1998, p. 28). The term is now being used more generally to denote children who are competent to make decisions for themselves independent from their parents and other adults (Dalrymple and Burke, 1995, p. xvi). It still remains an adult's decision whether a child is old enough and has sufficient understanding to make his or her own decisions. Adults often wish to protect children, believing that they know what is in a child's best interests and may find it hard to make the necessary adjustments as children grow older and become more independent. Despite the Gillick judgement, courts have taken the lead in continuing paternalism towards 'competent' children (Brandon, Schofield and Trinder, 1998, p. 32).

In endeavouring to achieve the highest feasible level of involvement of children, there is a tension as to who is in control, parent or child and in other situations, social workers or children. Despite sometimes being referred to as children's charter, The Children Act 1989 gave children few decision rights, as opposed to participation rights. Brandon, Schofield and Trinder (1998, p. 28) argue that even the right to participate is not consistently applied throughout the Act, with it depending on the child's age, level of maturity and the issue at stake. The question for day-to-day practice is when can children move beyond the *being consulted* level and become partners or be in control. With adults the presumption may be that they have the capacity to make life decisions for themselves unless a case can be made that they have not. The situation may be reversed for children, with the onus being on establishing that they have sufficient understanding to make particular decisions for themselves.

Incapacity to make decisions

Adults with severe dementia, a severe learning difficulty, a severe mental health problem or neurological damage may not have the capacity to make certain decisions for themselves or to negotiate decisions in partnership. A distinction can be drawn between legal provisions to protect people with a mental incapacity to make a particular decision and the day-to-day issues that arise for social workers, clients, carers and other stakeholders. There is a danger that decision incapacity is seen as a global attribute of clients, rather than only appertaining to a particular decision or type of decision. It may be that a specific decision needs to be taken for a person, if they lack the capacity to make that particular decision or type of decision, while they remain capable of making decisions in other areas for themselves. The basis on which such decisions are made can be an issue.

The basis can be what is considered in their *best interests* or by what is known as *substituted judgement* (Penhale, 1992, p. 187). Although it may be appropriate to take decisions in respect of younger children on what is considered their best interests, increasingly substituted judgement is seen as the appropriate basis for adults who have lost or never had the capacity to make certain decisions. Substituted judgement is deciding on the basis of what the individual would have chosen if they were still capable of exercising the choice. As was stressed previously, the lack of capacity to make a particular decision does not alter the need to involve clients to the highest possible level (O'Sullivan, 1990) which at the very least will be consultation. Making decisions for people who do not have the capacity to do so for themselves is a complex and problematic area of practice that needs the greatest of care, in which there may be a need for an independent advocate (Brandon, 1995, p. 42) and a more integrated legal framework than at present exists (BASW, 1998).

Fairly distributing limited resources

The third reason for restricting levels of involvement is the need to fairly distribute limited resources which are usually discussed in the context of people's needs. The example raises some complex issues about what constitutes need and how it is to be operationalised (for discussion of these, see Bradshaw, 1972; Wetherly, 1996). Space does not permit detailed discussion here, but it is useful to distinguish between three ways of establishing need: establishing client defined need by asking the empowered client, establishing professionally defined need by social workers using their professional judgement or establishing bureaucratically defined need by applying agency rules and procedures. The social worker is often in an intermediary position, carrying out agency policy and following agency procedure, while wanting to fulfil either the empowered client defined need or professionally defined need or some negotiated consensus between the two. Social workers may perceive that they have no choice but to reluctantly accept the level of resources that have been politically made available to them, and endeavour to do the best they can within these, while actively campaigning for more resources.

Who should determine the level of involvement?

Each of the parties – the client, social worker and agency – will have their own views as to what the level of involvement should be. It is possible to distinguish between four types of decision: client life decisions, agency resource decisions, service decisions and decisions to protect other people. It has been argued that the starting-point of any consideration should be that clients have control over decisions concerning their own bodies, lifestyles and actions. A move down to a lower level of involvement for these life decisions only becomes appropriate when either a strict criteria of incapacity has been met or having control puts a person in serious danger of harm. While decisions about the allocation of resources may need to be taken on a consultative basis, once made, service planning decisions can be made in partnership. Without rationing restrictions, clients could have control of resources to meet their expressed need but in the context of limited resources, definitions of need are used by agencies to prioritise need. As may turn out to be the case in the example, negotiating a consensus about allocation of resources may not be feasible in the context of finite resources and involvement may be restricted to consultation.

Clients will have their own views about what level of involvement in decision making they wish to have and a source of a dilemma for Sandra has become Ann not being at all keen on attending the review. She knows that unless during the course of the review the team manager changes her mind she will have to draw her work with Ann to a close. Sandra has come to believe the work should continue on a re-focused basis, but has been unable to convince her team manager. She has advocated on behalf of Ann without success and has come to believe that the only hope is for Ann to make a convincing case for herself at the review. Sandra is aware that if Ann competently presents herself at the review she may well undermine her own case for support, while at the same time any encouragement from Sandra to argue her own case may subject Ann to too much pressure too soon. Sandra very much believes in an open non-patronising approach and reminds herself that Ann is an adult and should be respected as such. She believes that with preparation for the review, Ann could become empowered to have control over her own participation and together they consider the various sources of disempowerment and how they could be overcome, but in the last analysis it will be for Ann to decide whether to attend the review or not.

Issues in Client Involvement

The third problematic area in involving clients in decision making concerns issues of client empowerment, which is a complex political process (see Rees, 1991, chapter 8) and space only permits the highlighting of certain features in relation to involvement in decision making. All the higher levels of involvement (being consulted, being a partner and being in control) may prove impossible without the client becoming empowered to involve themselves in decision making, but empowerment is by no means a straightforward or unproblematic idea. There are many issues around what is meant by empowerment, how clients become empowered and for what purpose (Adams, 1996b, p. 10) with a particular danger of clients becoming the victims rather than the beneficiaries of professional empowerment practice (see Bristow, 1994).

Co-operation or compliance

A common reason given by social workers for not involving clients is that they would not co-operate. A degree of co-operation is needed between social workers and clients, but care is needed to distinguish between co-operation and compliance. Emphasis needs to be placed on engaging clients in the process but co-operation is a two-edged sword which presents clients with a dilemma. If they unconditionally co-operate they may achieve some influence but at the cost of their autonomy. The more involved they become in agency decision making, potentially the more accountable they become to the agency. If they don't co-operate, they keep their autonomy but have no influence. Stephen Webb (1994) puts forward a third option of conditional co-operation that leaves clients less vulnerable to coercion and manipulation. Clients co-operate but are prepared to withdraw their co-operation at any point it ceases to be in their interest.

Empowerment and emancipation

There are similarities between the idea of empowerment and that of emancipation, but the latter places more emphasis on the clients breaking out of socially confined roles. The clients' position within an unequal society has implications for involving them in decision making as they are often members of the most powerless groups with restricted life-chances. Their powerlessness can be traced to the dominance of certain groups manifested in the existence of poverty:

ethnocentrism, sexism, ablism, ageism, racism and heterosexism. The individual social worker can do little directly about the client's position in society, but can engage in anti-oppressive practice at the institutional and structural levels (Rees, 1991; Dalrymple and Burke, 1995). They can also focus their work on clients becoming aware of the sources of their difficulties, facilitating their understanding of the power structures of society (see Freire, 1972) and so being able to liberate themselves from internalised oppression (Braye and Preston-Shoot, 1995, p. 109).

Such work may be more successful if the social worker and client share membership of an oppressed group. Sandra believes that part of Ann's problems is her oppressed position as a woman in a male-dominated society. Her individual work with her is a necessary first step (Hanmer and Statham, 1988, p. 129), after which Ann may wish to join a group within which she could raise her consciousness about how her position in society is contributing to her difficulties (Penfold and Walker, 1984, p. 218). Ann has begun to believe her problems reflect more her position as a woman in a patriarchal society than some internal inadequacy. The view of herself as a victim is giving way to a view of herself as having potential control over her life but the problem remains that she, and others like her, lack control over many of the circumstances of life that deprive her of opportunity.

Working across difference

Social worker and client will have points of similarity and difference, and in many ways Ann and Sandra are of similar social positions with them both being women of white European descent of similar age. The main difference between them is of class background, with Ann having been brought up in a working-class family, whereas Sandra's family of origin was middle class. There is also a regional difference between them, with Ann very much identifying with the north of the country and regarding Sandra, a southerner, with some suspicion. Sandra has managed to engage with Ann, but in the background lurks Ann's suspicion that Sandra regards herself as superior. Working across difference is a complex area given the existence of a number of different dimensions of oppression, their interwoven nature and the numerous permutations possible (see Narayan, 1989; Thompson, 1997, p. 12; Phillipson, 1992, p. 13). To take just three dimensions, being the same gender has a different impact than the social worker and client being of different genders. Likewise being members of the same ethnic group is different to being of dissimilar ethnicities or in the context of racism both having the same colour of skin is different from one being black and the other white.

As it is not practical (and probably not desirable) to match client and social worker on all the dimensions of oppression there will inevitably be differences between them. An aspect of anti-oppressive practice is social workers counteracting their own oppressive practices (see Phillipson, 1992; Dominelli, 1988), but they also need to have the skills and knowledge associated with communication across difference (Narayan, 1989). Narayan maintains that good will is not enough and non-members of oppressed groups should show humility and caution when communicating with members about their life and grant them epistemic privilege which 'amounts to claiming that members of an oppressed group have a more immediate, subtle and critical knowledge about the nature of their oppression than people who are non-members' (Narayan, 1989, p. 319). There are also practice implications when the social worker is a member of a subordinated group in relation to the client. For example, when a black social worker works with white client, there is the issue of not being disempowered by racism and being anti-racist in relation to the client in the context of the client's own position on the other dimensions of oppression. This will need to be in the context of an agency having a clear and effective policy for responding to racial harassment from white clients (Dominelli, 1988, p. 125).

Worker expertise and client empowerment

One of the contexts of involving clients in the making of decisions is the role given to experts in society, with there being a trend towards people handing over more and more aspects of their lives to the regulation of experts (see Illich *et al.*, 1977). Despite Sandra's best efforts, Ann may continue to put Sandra in a position of authority based on her real or perceived powers and expertise. The image of social workers as authority figures may have been well established long before Sandra came into contact with Ann, who continues to see Sandra as an expert from whom she seeks a solution to her problem. In these circumstances, an integral part of the work is clients liberating themselves from these beliefs, with a start being made by exploring the beliefs themselves. Nevertheless recognition needs to be given to the fact that the professional role does carry authority and it can be hardly surprising that clients get confused. One minute the social worker may claim the right to intervene, the next that clients need to be responsible for their own lives.

Agency support and worker empowerment

Both the practice of the social worker and the policy and procedures of the agency need to actively promote client involvement (Beresford and Croft, 1993). This means that there needs to be a proactive stance, with positive encouragement and a carefully thought-out policy designed to overcome the barriers to client involvement. This will include training, consultation and support for the staff of the agency. Whether an agency is specifically geared to promoting client involvement or not, the client can remain powerless in relation to the overwhelming power of the agency. Both social workers and their agencies can find themselves under severe constraints outside their influence which can mean that even where there is strong motivation they may not be able to achieve high levels of client involvement and pressure for change will need to come from oppositional groups outside the agency (Forbes and Sashidharan, 1997).

A social worker who feels disempowered will not be able to work positively towards client involvement (Baldwin, 1990, p. 185). Within particular organisational environments disempowerment may manifest itself as worker burnout, low staff morale or the development of a siege mentality. High levels of client involvement are enabled by social workers having a strong professional identity, good working practices, sound skills and valid knowledge base. Social workers need to have both the motivation and the ability to promote client involvement but no matter how able and how well motivated, if their agencies are not committed or organised to promote client involvement, they will face an uphill struggle. A strong professional identity and alliances with client groups will help in these circumstances, but the individual social worker is in a vulnerable position and may need the support of a strong campaigning professional association.

How is the Client to Become Empowered?

As well as being concerned with the way society, agencies and professional practice can oppress and disempower clients, social workers also need to be concerned with clients overcoming the effects of past and present oppression which can present barriers to clients becoming involved (Adams, 1996b, p. 61). Issues need to be addressed if the client is to participate effectively in decision making which may include whether they have the information they need, sufficient emotional energy, confidence in their ability and belief that they can make a difference. Sandra is working with Ann on an individual basis, which may not be as effective as her joining a group with others in a similar position (see Mullender and Ward, 1991). There is also the issue of whether it would be better if Ann had an advocate (see Brandon, 1995) to speak for her at the review rather than the client empowerment approach preferred by Sandra.

The need for information

The need for clients to have information is an issue at all levels of involvement as they will not always know what is possible and may content themselves with the familiar. As Morrison indicated, 'people want what they know rather than know what they want' (Morrison, 1988, p. 207). If clients are to be involved in decision making they will need accessible information about services, life issues, policy and procedures to be able to take an informed view of the decision situation and the options available. What is meant by an informed view can be problematic, with one person's informed view being another person's biased or mistaken view. The social worker has a responsibility to increase the clients' awareness of what could be available but where clients get their information can be an issue. The agency has a responsibility to provide accessible information, but clients may also need access to independent sources of information, advice and advocacy services.

Recognising and working with emotions

Account needs to be taken of 'the emotional cost of a life which has been directed by other people or fashioned by uncontrollable circumstances' (Barber, 1991, p. 35) which may result in an understandable reluctance to be involved (Croft and Beresford, 1993, p.

30). Clients may feel emotionally drained and actually want decisions made for them, feeling already overburdened by life, without
the further burden of being involved in decision making. The social
worker needs to be cautious about rushing to take responsibility, as
there is a danger that this will only confirm the client's self-image as
'inadequate'. Inexperienced social workers may mistakenly see their
role as solving the client's problems for them rather than working
with them to regain some control over their lives. Ann decides to
attend the review but as she gets anxious about attending meetings
she would rather Sandra spoke on her behalf. Sandra resists the
temptation to take over, but is aware that there is a balance to be
struck between encouraging Ann to speak and putting her under
undue pressure which would be counter-productive. An important
part of Sandra's role is to support Ann without further disempow-
ering her and they arrange two meetings together to specifically
prepare for the review. Whether Sandra is successful in striking the
right balance will depend on her sensitivity to the issues involved
and how she manages them.

Building confidence

Clients may lack confidence in their own ability to contribute to the
making of decisions – something that can often be traced back to
the low self-esteem or lack of life skills associated with their
positions in society. Preparation in the form of having clear
accessible information, further education or rehearsal opportunities
can contribute to the overcoming of these beliefs and the development of new skills. Support from family members, friends, client
groups, community groups or independent agencies may also be
needed. Clients may have had life-long experiences of being dis-
counted and ignored, and may have missed out on the opportunities
to develop themselves. Some compensation for these negative
experiences may be needed to enable clients to gain confidence in
themselves. In the case example, Ann left school at the earliest
opportunity without any qualifications and has been undermined
all her life by male partners and her father. As a consequence she
lacks confidence in her own ability to present her case at the review,
something that will be a new experience for her. Fear of the
unknown can be very disabling and Sandra takes care to show
Ann the room in which the review will take place and introduces her
to the team manager so as to be familiar with these before the day of

the review. During the preparation meetings, Sandra rehearses with Ann what will happen at the review and what she wants to say.

Restoring hope

Hope that things can get better provides an important motivation to participate in decision making, but the absence of hope is often a symptom of disempowerment. Hope can be related both to the client's psychological state and his or her perception of external conditions which may more or less relate to how things actually are. For example, the lack of hope of getting a job may be related to a realistic appraisal of the current employment situation, leaving the restoration of hope dependent on the employment situation changing. In other circumstances, lack of hope may relate more to the client's beliefs or emotions, with the gaining of hope dependent on these changing. In many decision situations the combination of internal and external factors may contribute to a lack of hope. One issue in the restoration of hope is the danger of kindling false hope. Ann has little hope that Sandra's team manager will change her mind and Sandra is in two minds about Ann becoming more hopeful about the outcome of the review. She knows that false hope can be very destructive and she examines the basis of her own hope, concluding that there will be authentic consultation at the review. She believes that her team manager is still open to influence and has not closed her mind to the possibility that the work with Ann could continue.

The team manager does not change her mind but Ann gets a certain amount of satisfaction from putting her own case forward and feels she has made the first crucial step in gaining some control over her life. In the end pressure from what was perceived as higher-priority work determined the result with a negotiated agreement proving unattainable. The level of involvement turned out to be *being consulted*, with the team manager carefully taking into account the arguments put forward by Ann and Sandra. Sandra is disappointed with the decision of the review and wonders whether it is worth struggling on, facing set-back after set-back in her quest to promote preventative work She feels undermined by her team manager who she believes could have had more respect for her professional judgement as to what was needed in Ann's situation. She hopes Ann maintains her recovery, but fears that the team will be seeing Ann again but this time as a high-priority referral.

CHAPTER SUMMARY AND KEY POINTS

It has been argued that clients need to be involved in decision making in social work, and this chapter considered the issues and possible levels of client involvement. The question of who the client is was addressed and four levels of involvement identified. The factors that influence the level of involvement were discussed, including issues of client protection, the protection of others, the incapacity of some clients to make a particular decision and the need for agencies to ration resources. The chapter finished by considering the elements of an empowering practice to overcome the barriers to involvement, including the legacy of a life lived in poverty and other forms of oppression.

When involving the client to the highest possible level, the following points need to be considered:

- who the client/s are;
- what level of involvement is being aimed for;
- whether this is the highest level of involvement feasible; and
- how this level of involvement can be achieved.

The tensions and issues when involving the client in decision making include:

- the potentially differing perspectives of primary and secondary clients;
- reconciling the need for client protection and client autonomy; and
- how to facilitate client empowerment without actually confirming the client's powerless position.

4

Stakeholders Meeting Together

A characteristic of sound decision making is stakeholders consulting with each other so that differing perspectives can be taken into account. This may involve stakeholders (including the client/s) meeting together to discuss the decision situation. While this gives rise to certain opportunities, there is also the danger that the client will feel intimidated while other stakeholders dominate the proceedings. Social work practice needs to be geared to facilitating stakeholders to work together in a constructive way but issues of power mean that achieving the full benefits of meeting together remains a formidable challenge.

ILLUSTRATIVE EXAMPLE

Ellen is a child care social worker about to attend a review in respect of John, a four-year-old who is the subject of a care order and is currently placed with foster parents. He has been in the care of the local authority for four months. The care order was made after a series of incidents in which John was left alone by his mother and her partner. John was regarded as suffering from general neglect and there were also a number of unexplained injuries. Gail now has a new partner and wants her son back home. Ellen has carried out a comprehensive assessment of Gail and her new partner and is proposing a child care plan that involves John being placed with his mother while still being subject to the care order. The review will consider whether the proposal will meet John's needs and provide for his safety.

Who Needs to Meet Together?

Who is actually present when stakeholders meet together is one of the factors shaping what happens at the meeting. There are the twin dangers of indiscriminately inviting as many people as possible in an attempt to relieve the anxiety generated by the decision situation and of excluding or overlooking key people. The co-ordinator, who may or may not be the social worker, needs to consider with the client a number of issues in relation to who will be invited and who will attend, including the identification of stakeholders, the appropriateness of them meeting together, the type of meeting it will be and who has a valid reason for being present.

Who are stakeholders?

Stakeholder is a term being used to denote those who have an interest in the decision situation. In any one decision situation there is potentially a long list of stakeholders. These range from central figures to peripheral ones, including the clients, members of the clients' immediate and extended families and communities, members of professional and non-professional networks involved with the clients, social workers and social work managers, and sometimes agencies that have a particular responsibility but who have no direct involvement. If all the people who could be identified as stakeholders were invited to the meeting, it would most likely be too large for useful discussion and exchanges to take place. Rather than trying to draw up an exhaustive list of who could be invited, careful consideration needs to be given to who, out of the pool of stakeholders, have valid reasons for being present to discuss the particular decision in question.

Do stakeholders need to meet together?

Meeting together every time a decision needs to be made is not feasible or desirable and is indicated when interaction between the various stakeholders is required to resolve the decision situation. The trade-off between the cost of meeting together in terms of time and energy and the potential benefits mean that stakeholder meetings may need to be reserved for critical decisions that represent turning-points in the decision situation. These will tend to be planning decisions, decisions responding to newly acquired critical information and review decisions. In some circumstances it may be enough for stakeholders to be consulted separately as individuals, but a different quality is brought to these consultations when they actually meet together and have the benefit of hearing what the others have to say.

What type of meeting will it be?

John's review is just one of many types of meeting in social work in which two or more stakeholders sit down together to discuss decisions. Decision making meetings can be divided into more formal meetings, like reviews, conferences, committees and panels, and less formal meetings, like supervision sessions, interviews and discussions of various other kinds. Sometimes stakeholders meet together as part of a more formal procedure that needs to be complied with, while at other times the social worker needs to be proactive in drawing stakeholders together to discuss a decision as in a family network meeting or case conference. John's review is being held under the Review of Children's Cases Regulations 1991 and so falls into the category of a more formal meeting between stakeholders and so there is less discretion over who is invited. The regulations require that as far as it is practicable the child and his or her parents be involved, as well as any other person whose views are considered relevant (Regulation 7(2)). In addition, the official guidance states that the child's carer be invited (Department of Health, 1991c, p. 83).

Who needs to be present?

There is a tension between the need to be inclusive and the need to create the conditions in which constructive discussions can take place. Large meetings can be intimidating and can have demotivating effects (see Baron *et al.*, 1992, chapter 4) with stakeholders leaving the responsibility of contributing to others. There is less opportunity to make contributions in larger groups, particularly when there is competition over who speaks next. The negative consequences of large meetings may mean that only those who have a particular reason for being present will be invited. A valid reason may be that their expertise, commitment, backing, information, resources or support is required if a sound decision is to be made or, alternatively, that they have the right to be present as a matter of principle.

Given the need for differing perspectives to come into the picture, meetings in social work tend to be larger than they otherwise would ideally be. Nine people will be present at John's review. This will include the health visitor and paediatrician, who were members of the child protection review conference that removed John's name from the child protection register after he was made the subject of a care order. John's foster parents, Gail and her new partner and John will also be present. If the whereabouts of John's father had been known, he would have also been invited. The review is to be chaired by the area manager and Ellen will be present as the key worker. The attendance of children at reviews and conferences can be an issue and the subject of some disagreement. Minty argues that 'the current practice in many agencies of making it a rule that older children participate in large meetings, such as case conferences, where the inadequacies of their families may be publicly exposed' is insensitive (Minty, 1995, p. 49). Given John's young age there was some discussion about whether it was appropriate for him to be present for the whole of the review, as some of the discussion would concern the behaviour of his mother (see Thoburn, Lewis and Shemmings, 1995, p. 232) but it was decided that with certain safeguards he would be present.

Who will attend?

As well as the issue of who to invite, there is the issue of who will attend. It is not uncommon for important members of the professional or family network to be unable or unwilling to attend a meeting. If the paediatrician or Gail's new partner had been unable or unwilling to attend, important perspectives would have been missing from the meeting. A recurrent theme of research into child protection conferences is the absence of the family's GP (Hallett, 1995, p. 178) and it is not uncommon for a particular family member to refuse to attend a family network meeting. Professional stakeholders may be considered to have a responsibility to attend, but non-professional stakeholders, including clients, have the right to choose not to attend and my have good reasons for doing so. The effect of having a missing member can vary between those present doing the best they can in the absence of a particular stakeholder to the business of the meeting remaining incomplete. Missing stakeholders can also become convenient scapegoats on which to deposit negative feelings.

Issues of Power Between Stakeholders

Power is an important but problematic area when stakeholders meet together. Such meetings have formal and informal structures, that reflect institutional arrangements and the inequalities in society. These structures represent both impediments to stakeholders working together and the reality of the challenge of making decisions in social work. A fear is that the meeting will be dominated by certain individuals, sub-groups or interests and other stakeholders will not have an effective say. A key aim of social work practice is to empower all stakeholders to participate, despite differences in power. If this aim is to have a chance of being achieved there needs to be a clear understanding of the issues of power that meeting together entails. There is a danger that decisions will be taken by those who have the power to do so even before the meeting starts, leaving other stakeholders without influence. For example, the area manager and Ellen could have had discussions before the review and agreed that John be placed with his mother leaving the review as a ritualistic set piece in which their decisions are 'rubber stamped'. There is a legitimate need for the various stakeholders to have pre-meeting discussions, particularly in terms of preparing for the meeting, but there is clearly a distinction to be made between necessary preparations and the usurping of a meeting's decision making role.

Authority or oppression

A distinction can be drawn between the legitimate use of power, which within social work is regarded as *authority*, and the illegitimate use of power which can be termed *oppression*. Beetham defines legitimate power as being 'acquired and exercised according to justifiable rules and with evidence of consent' (Beetham, 1991, p. 3). It is restricted to specified socially or organisationally sanctioned areas connected to a position held within an organisation or an official role. The notion of legitimate power is problematic and which aspects of power reflect authority and which are to be regarded as oppression can be an issue. The distinction between authority and oppression is made more complex by the fact that legitimate power can be misused or mis-directed, and can spill over into areas for which there is no mandate. Even when legitimate power is used within its mandated area in a competent and appropriate manner, not everybody will accept its legitimacy with there being a distinction between social legitimation and individual legitimation.

Structures of authority mean that many meetings within social work will have hierarchical elements to them. Not everybody agrees that this is the way things have to be or should be (Iannello, 1992), but the reality that confronts individual social workers are hierarchical groups. The power of the area manager within John's review can be regarded as legitimate, it being based on her organisational position and legal requirements. She is chairing the review with delegated authority from the director to make decisions concerning the placement of children on care orders with their parents (Placement of Children with Parents etc. Regulations, 1991). Her authority to make this decision needs to be exercised in a proper manner or else it will lose its legitimacy. It may not always be possible to so neatly delineate between authority and oppression as they can become entangled with each other. Meeting together can lay bare the inequalities of power that have no legitimacy and those stakeholders who are already in a powerless position can have this compounded at the meeting.

Discrimination or appreciation

Social groups may have power by virtue of their dominant position in society. These patterns of dominance can vary between societies, being subject to change and reflecting social structures of oppression. If a member of a socially subordinated group is substantially outnumbered by members of a socially dominant group they can feel isolated and intimidated. This is particularly so if the meeting is not conducted in the client's first language, a situation only partly ameliorated by the provision of appropriate interpretation and translation services (Dominelli, 1997b, p. 106). Even when members of socially powerful groups are in a minority, they can still exercise power through their dominant social position. Whether social power is exercised by individuals or sub-groups, anti-oppressive practice is an important aspect of participating in a meeting between stakeholders and issues of inequality in respect of gender, 'race', ethnicity, age, ability, sexuality, language and religion need to be taken into account (Adams and O'Sullivan, 1994, p. 38).

Difference needs to be a source of appreciation for the richness and variety it brings to society rather than a source of fear and discrimination. In practice members of society who are perceived to be different are often discriminated against by members of dominant groups. To the extent that the stakeholders meeting together form a microcosm of the wider society, there is likely to be a replication of the social structures of oppression within the group, with members and non-members of oppressed groups being present. In her discussion of the issues involved in working across difference, Narayan (1989) refers to members of a particular oppressed group as *insiders* and non-members as *outsiders*. This distinction needs to be used with some care since there are many dimensions of oppression and people are insiders only in respect of a specific form of oppression. This means that a person can be an insider in respect of one oppressed group but an outsider in respect of another. There is also a distinction between outsiders who are sympathetic to the insiders' cause and those who are, either through lack of awareness or explicit conviction, indifferent or hostile. Communicating across differences is a necessary but problematic process, as the power relations between insiders and outsiders have been historically constructed and 'the presence of goodwill on the part the outsiders is not enough to overcome assumptions and attitudes born out of centuries of power and privilege' (Narayan, 1989, p. 319). An example of complexity in this area is the issue of a sympathetic outsider challenging discriminatory views of another outsider in the presence of an insider.

Individual stakeholders may hold racist, sexist, ageist, ethnocentric, homophobic, or ablist views and make discriminatory comments. In the long term these attitudes and beliefs need to be confronted, but it will depend on the actual circumstances of a meeting as to whether and how such discrimination is challenged and by whom. Insiders have the right to speak for themselves and not be subjected to patronising attempts by sympathetic outsiders to speak for them, but the very nature of these meetings is that insiders can be isolated and often not in a position to speak for themselves. It may fall to sympathetic outsiders to challenge discriminatory views and they need to take into account the likely effect of their challenge on both the insider and the offending outsider. Any comments made need to be sensitive and not make a bad situation worse for the insider, by embarrassing them with well-intentioned but clumsy interventions or the outsider by provoking a defensive reaction that may compound their discriminatory attitudes. Insiders have the right to speak with anger when confronted with discrimination, but a sympathetic outsider may take into account the effect of their challenge on the offending outsider. Confrontation and challenging can be associated with a harsh attacking activity, but need to include gentle but firm discussion with people directed at promoting awareness (Compton and Galaway, 1989, p. 185).

Influence or domination

One reason for stakeholders to meet together is to have the opportunity to influence the decision, but influence can easily become domination. It is the manner or method of influence that is important. To influence can be defined as to affect a person's point of view or action in a particular direction. Charles Handy (1985, p.129) identifies methods of influence as including physical force, rules and procedures, exchange, persuasion and manipulation of the environment. Although all these may operate within social work, the term influence will be used in a restricted sense of referring to persuasion, that is, stakeholders changing their minds or actions by being convinced of the reasoned arguments of others. The term domination will be used to denote changes not freely entered into by a fully informed stakeholder, the crucial difference being the degree to which stakeholders feel under duress or compulsion to accept the other's point of view. The health visitor does not believe Gail will cope if John returns home. Ellen endeavours to influence the health visitor's attitude towards Gail by explaining how much progress she has made since her son has been away from her. The health visitor needs to become convinced that the situation has moved on rather than being provoked into an obstinate resistance.

Observers or participants

Some stakeholders may be denied the opportunity to influence the decision, even though they are present (Corby, Millar and Young, 1994), and there is a danger that clients and other non-professionals are left as observers rather than being participants at the meeting. This relates to one of the sharpest divisions of power, being between those that hold official positions and those that do not. Gail and her new partner and to a lesser extent John's foster parents, are likely to feel at a disadvantage in the room full of professionals and may be inhibited from expressing their opinions. In these circumstances, anti-oppressive practice and empowering practice have important roles to play in achieving the goal of participation. This would include careful choice of venue, the use of non-technical language (Pugh, 1996, p. 88), putting people at their ease, fully explaining procedures and encouraging people to participate. Chapter 3 showed that considerable preparatory work may be required before clients feel able to become involved. John is the primary client and as a child he is in a potentially even more disadvantageous position. Ellen has had the responsibility to prepare John for the review and present his wishes and feelings to the meeting. It is open to question whether she is in a position to do so effectively and it has been argued that this is a role for an independent advocate (Scutt, 1995).

Peers or professional hierarchy

Relations between the different professions are ideally based on mutual respect for each other's particular expertise. Unfortunately, this is not always the case and certain professions can occupy dominant positions, potentially leaving some stakeholders feeling either intimidated or without influence. The perspectives of the different professions can carry different weights – for example, male professions being given more weight than female professions (Ferguson, 1987; Stevenson, 1989, p. 185). This does not relate to the gender of individual members of these professions, but rather their professional ethos which is rooted in their histories. Medical perspectives and legal perspectives (both of which have a predominantly male ethos) can carry more weight than social work perspectives or nursing perspectives which have a more female ethos. Professional ethos may be counterbalanced by other factors, such as a stakeholder's agency being the lead agency or the controller of resources.

Potential Benefits of Meeting Together

The total amount of person-hours taken up by a meeting can be obtained by multiplying the duration of the meeting by the number of people involved. When looked at in this way meetings use up considerable amounts of time. This represents a significant investment that will only be justified if the potential benefits of meeting together are realised. These potential benefits include the develop-ment of: a fuller picture; a new synthesis; co-ordinated action; and commitment to carrying out the decision.

A fuller picture or partial view

One of the potential benefits of stakeholders meeting together is to share information that enables a fuller picture to be developed rather than each of the stakeholders having a separate partial view. This is one reason for the introduction of child protection confer-ences. Inquiry reports, such as the one into the death of Maria Colwell (DHSS, 1974), pinpointed the lack of shared information between agencies as a reason why children have not been protected and adults at risk have been involved in tragedies. It was believed that if all the bits of the jigsaw had been put together then decisive action could have been taken. However, information sharing is not a straightforward mechanical process. The information contributed needs to be sorted and evaluated (London Borough of Lambeth, 1987, p. 151) and simply meeting together does not ensure that effective communication will take place (Reder, Duncan and Gray, 1993, p. 67). Nevertheless, with appropriate facilitation a meeting between stakeholders can produce a much richer and more valid picture of the decision situation compared with that which existed before the meeting. This can include a fuller assessment of the nature of the problem, what is required and what can be done, with the potential that access is gained to sources of support which may not have been available if stakeholders had not met together.

A new synthesis or a compromise

A potential benefit of meeting together is that the differing views of stakeholders can be shared and combined to form a new synthesis that is more developed than its constituent views. Rather than being a source of conflict, differing views can be used creatively to build upon each other to produce new ways of looking at the decision situation. The health visitor and paediatrician are concerned about John being returned to his mother, but Ellen believes that the plan is in John's best interests. Coming out of these two opposing views is the possibility of a new synthesis that has the backing of the entire group. An example of a new synthesis would be John returning home, but his name being reinstated on the child protection register.

A new synthesis is different from a compromise in which the participants perceive the decision result as a concession rather than a new insight. An example of a compromise would be for John to spend each alternate week with his mother. With a compromise each side gives a little so as to meet the other in the middle, potentially producing an unsound decision that satisfies no one. Seeking a compromise may be used as a way of dissipating conflict, with stakeholders coming under considerable pressure to make concessions. By contrast, a new synthesis is produced by the differences being discussed openly rather than them being rapidly closed down at the first sign of conflict.

Co-ordinated or isolated actions

If stakeholders meet together there is the opportunity for them to co-ordinate their actions rather than work in isolation from each other. This can involve either each individual stakeholder, adjusting his or her own plans in the light of what the others are doing, or the development of an overall plan to which they all work. Many decisions require joint and co-ordinated implementation; for example, John's foster parents need to place their work with John and his mother in the context of an overall plan, something they will be able to do more effectively if they have been a party to the discussion. The plan for John's return would also have implications for the work of the health visitor. The health and social services need to be integrated services, so that their staff can work together in a co-ordinated and dovetailed manner, each supportive of the other. If stakeholders meet together, they can make sure that what each of them does fits in with what the other is doing, thereby giving more chance of decisions being successfully implemented.

Commitment or compliance

John's successful return home would need the commitment of all those involved. One of the potential benefits of meeting together is that the various stakeholders can come to share a commitment to a plan. The foster parents would play an important role in John's successful return home and if they remain unconvinced of the merits of the plan they may comply with it but have no commitment to it. Commitment stems from feeling a party to the decision rather than having it imposed; if the foster parents have their point of view listened to and taken into account, they are more likely to have commitment to what is decided. Mere presence is not enough for this to take place but rather actual participation. Commitment can be enhanced when explicitly expressed in the presence of others. It is known from research that individuals tend to have more commitment to carrying out a decision if they declare their intention publicly rather than keeping it to themselves (Janis and Mann, 1977, p. 281). So if it is decided at the review to adopt the plan for John's return home, and the various stakeholders publicly agree to this, there is likely to be greater commitment than if they had not expressed their agreement during the meeting.

Achieving the Potential Benefits of Meeting Together

There can be very different consequences of consulting in groups, reflected in the two expressions, 'two heads are better than one' and 'a camel is a horse designed by committee' (Vroom and Jago, 1988, p. 20). The chances of the potential benefits of stakeholders meeting together being realised are increased by the presence of a number of facilitating processes. These include: preparing for the meeting, skilful chairing, stakeholder participation, the development of a co-operative group climate, vigilant listening, maintaining focused discussion and constructive management of conflict. The absence of these processes may not only mean that an unsound decision is made but that the investment of the time of a number of people has not been justified and an opportunity has been lost. Worse still, what Morrison refers to as 'unhealthy processes' can operate when something that is happening under the 'table ... is dominating whatever is going on across it' (Morrison, 1993, p. 91).

Preparing for the meeting

If stakeholders are to successfully meet together the meeting will need certain preparations. In order to prepare themselves social workers may have a series of discussions with the different stakeholders before the meeting. Ellen has been involved in a number of pre-review discussions. She has consulted with her team, her line manager, specialist advisors in law and child protection, the health visitor, Gail, her new partner, John's foster parents and John. The preparatory work with clients and other non-professional stakeholders has the added importance of placing Ellen in a better position to facilitate their participation if they feel intimidated or overwhelmed by the meeting. Work with children before child care reviews is particularly important because the review needs to take into account their wishes and feelings. This does not necessarily mean talking on their behalf at the review, but will involve making sure they understand that they do not have to speak and preparing with them anything they do wish to say (Scutt, 1995, p. 238).

Skilful chairing

The chair of the meeting plays a crucial role in facilitating stake-holders to work together in a constructive and vigilant way. This involves enabling stakeholders to discuss the decision situation and to maintain positive working relationships with one another. There can be considerable variation in the way the role of chair is carried out. For example, the chair can contribute to the discussion in a direct way by putting a view forward or restrict herself to asking exploratory questions, and reflecting and synthesising the group discussion. There are a number of aspects of chairing a meeting – for example, there is often a strong emotional content to the decisions that need to be made within social work. An important role of the chair is enabling these emotions to be expressed without them disabling the group. Considerable skill is needed to enable each stakeholder to participate without important issues being sidetracked for fear of strong emotions being expressed and so preventing the premature closure of the discussion. The responsi-bility of facilitating stakeholders working together also falls upon other stakeholders, particularly those who have a professional or family responsibility.

Promoting participation

The purpose of gathering stakeholders together is not so that they can observe the proceedings but to be participants. To participate is to make a contribution that is listened to and taken into account in the group's deliberations. If a stakeholder's view coincides with that of the currently prevailing view in the meeting this can be a relatively straightforward matter. However, there is a danger that a stakeholder may keep quiet when his or her view differs. They may fear conflict, ridicule or chastisement, or lack the confidence to put a differing view forward. Gail has been invited to her son's review and intends to be present but the question remains as to how far she will be a participant. It is her choice if she wishes to speak, but she does need to have the opportunity and to feel that what she has to say will be respected and listened to. Whether Gail is able to put her point of view forward may depend on a number of factors, including her degree of confidence, how prepared she has been for the review and the degree of skill the chair and others, including Ellen, can bring to bear on enabling, facilitating and empowering her participation. Professional workers' participation may also need facilitation – for example, if the health visitor keeps her concerns to herself many of the benefits of meeting together will be lost. Exploratory questions from the chair may enable and encourage stakeholders to express their views, the general atmosphere being one in which each stakeholder's contribution is valued and actively sought.

Maintaining focused discussion

It is through discussion that potentially an in-depth picture of the decision situation is constructed, and a full range of appropriate options identified and appraised. Discussion involves the exchange of ideas, perspectives and opinions and may need to be encouraged in the search for different ways of looking at things. It is through the process of discussion that views are modified, abandoned, clarified or confirmed. Discussion may at times be a taken-for-granted process, but productive discussion is by no means inevitable and may need facilitation. If stakeholders are to make progress, discussion needs to be focused on the issues at hand and to take place in a logical sequence. While there may be no shortage of discussion, much of it can be off the point. The chair has a particular role facilitating group discussion that is focused on relevant issues and not letting the meeting become sidetracked on irrelevancies, but there is a balance to be struck between a stifling tight control on what is discussed and re-establishing the focus when the discussion drifts off on a tangent.

Vigilant listening

Vigilance on the part of stakeholders involves scrutinising the information and views put forward and challenging any inaccuracies. Meeting together enables the basis of decisions to be opened to scrutiny, but processes can operate that mean a stakeholder may feel unable to question the views of others. Ellen will put forward the proposal to place John with his mother. There is the danger that other members of the review will uncritically accept this plan at face value. To avoid this potential collusion, the other stakeholders may need to be encouraged to examine the plan and its justification. Ellen needs to be able to give a sound and convincing analysis of the situation that critically examines the factors in favour of John returning home and those against. Her proposal will need to be reconsidered if she cannot clearly demonstrate that John's placement with his mother is in his best interests. All stakeholders need to be vigilant as regards the views being put forward by the other stakeholders. For example, Gail carefully listens to what the foster parents say when they are critical of how she is with John when she visits. She believes that they are not taking sufficiently into account the difficulties involved in visiting your child when he is in somebody else's care and reminds them that they have only seen her when she visits him in *their* home and that she is very different with him when he has home visits.

Creating a co-operative group climate

A climate of co-operation, collaboration and mutual support needs to be created if stakeholders are to work together constructively. Establishing and emphasising a common purpose may help create such a climate. For example, the chair emphasises that stakeholders share the goal of promoting John's welfare, while there may be differences about how this can best be achieved. Such differences are important from a decision making point of view, but whether conflict takes place in a co-operative or competitive atmosphere will largely determine whether the conflict is constructive or destructive. The healthy exchange of differing opinions in the context of endeavouring to achieve a consensus is different from individual stakeholders or factions being embroiled in personal feuds, infighting or win/lose arguments. A group climate that values positive engagement in discussion, rather than active or passive destruction, can be fostered by enabling stakeholders, who hold differing views, to see each other as partners endeavouring to achieve consensus, rather than opponents trying to win the argument.

Constructive management of conflict

As already indicated, there are going to be a number of different points of view at John's review. The distinct perspectives of the various professional groups can be important sources of differing views (Øvretveit, 1993, p. 139), as can the different viewpoints of managers, professionals, family members and clients. Ellen is putting forward a care plan that involves John being placed with his mother while still on a care order. The paediatrician and health visitor believe this to be too risky, feeling that John needs to remain where he is. This view is supported by his foster parents. John remaining with his foster parents is not an available option, as far as Ellen is concerned, since the foster parents are only approved for short-term placements. Gail believes it is not necessary for the care order to remain in force when John comes home and wants the department to apply for its discharge. The area manager is not over-happy about children being placed with their parents while still on a care order; if John were to return home, she would rather that an application for the discharge of the care order were made.

If the benefits of meeting together are going to be realised, these differences need to be managed positively or they will be a source of destruction rather than creativity. Johnson and Johnson identified three negative strategies and three positive strategies used by individual stakeholders to manage conflict (Johnson and Johnson, 1982, p. 325). The three negative strategies are win–lose, rejection and avoidance. Win–lose involves viewing differences of opinion as an opportunity to win an argument at the expense of the other person. Rejection involves perceiving a member's disagreement as a personal rejection and so withdrawing from the discussion feeling hurt. Avoidance is evading arguments almost at any price. The three positive strategies are confirmation, perspective taking and problem solving. Confirmation involves confirming the other person as a valued person who you happen to disagree with on a particular point. Perspective taking involves seeing differences of opinion as opportunities to gain a different perspective on the issue. Problem solving involves endeavouring to bring differing perspectives together to form a new synthesis. It is through these positive strategies that conflict can be creative.

Agreement in meetings may be more common than expected, which from the perspective of creative use of conflict is a cause of concern rather than satisfaction. For example, one of the surprising findings of child protection research is the high degree of inter-agency agreement at child protection conferences (Hallett, 1995, p. 223; Farmer and Owen, 1995, p. 98), but care does need to be taken in distinguishing between agreement between the professionals and agreement between all stakeholders including the clients. There is a danger that when clients and professionals disagree, but the professionals agree between themselves, this is still taken as consensus – which of course it is not. The crucial processes of discussion and participation depend at least partly on the existence of differences of opinion, without which little can be achieved but the sharing of information that simply confirms the dominant view. As will be discussed, there can be a number of reasons why disagreement is hidden beneath the surface, including stakeholders being content to allow the lead agency to take responsibility, or when clients are solely seen as targets of persuasion rather than holders of points of view that need to be taken seriously (see Farmer and Owen, 1995, p. 108).

Seeking a Consensus

One view is that most benefit can be obtained from meeting together if a consensus is sought, as opposed to a compromise or majority view (Moscovici and Doise, 1994). This has less to do with the desirability of achieving a consensus per se and more to do with the processes that stem from striving to achieve a consensus. When seeking a consensus, each stakeholder's viewpoint needs to be established and differences not brushed aside. Even if consensus is not achieved the meeting can still have benefited from the processes triggered by endeavouring to achieve a consensus, which includes clarifying differences between views. Although the processes of endeavouring to achieve a consensus are considered to be conducive to working together, care is needed that they are not confused with those of unanimity or conformity.

Consensus is different from unanimity or conformity

As defined by Schein, a consensus exists when there is a clear option that most stakeholders subscribe to and 'communications have been sufficiently open, and the group climate has been sufficiently supportive, to make everyone in the group feel that he [sic] has had his [sic] fair chance to influence the decision' (Schein, 1988, p. 73). The important point in this definition is that those stake-holders who would *not* take the majority option as their first choice, feel they have had their chance to influence the decision and are prepared to support it. With consensus, all stakeholders have a degree of commitment to the decision because they feel they have been given a chance to influence it. When the term consensus is used in the way Schein suggests, it can be distinguished from unanimity and conformity.

If John's review was to decide on the basis of unanimity, it would be taken on the basis that all stakeholders agreed on the course of action to be taken, reflecting a uniform view held by all stake-holders. A distinction can be drawn between apparent unanimity and true unanimity. True unanimity is found in homogeneous groups that do not contain differences of opinion. A disadvantage of such groups is the lack of critical scrutiny and creativity that is associated with having differing views. Apparent unanimity occurs when on the surface it appears that all stakeholders agree, but in reality some or all are superficially conforming to a dominant view that they do not actually hold or that they find it convenient to acquiesce to. Such conformity can often take the form of silence rather than active support. Stakeholders can experience pressure to conform from a variety of sources that have little to do with the merits or otherwise of the case being put forward. They can con-form for a number of reasons; because they feel intimidated; because they lack confidence in their own view; because they fear conflict or fear upsetting others; or they may believe individually they are alone in their opposition, when in fact it is only one or two vocal stakeholders that hold the prevailing view. An extreme pressure to conform is referred to as groupthink and occurs in insular and cohesive groups in which all disagreement is suppressed (Janis, 1972).

The process of seeking a consensus

Endeavouring to achieve a consensus involves each stakeholder keeping their view under review while putting it forward for consideration by the meeting. Consensus can only be achieved when stakeholders are prepared to move forward in their view, building on the views expressed by others. This will not happen if stake-holders have rigid views that they are not prepared to change, no matter how convincing the counter arguments put forward. At the same time, changing one's view without good reason, as has been discussed, can be part of conformity. Consensus depends on stakeholders not being too ready to change their minds but doing so when convinced by argument or evidence. Ellen feels under pressure to accept that John needs to remain with his foster parents. However, she rejects this view believing that it is not based on a critical appraisal of the situation. Nevertheless she becomes more cautious in her approach to John being placed with his mother having listened to what the health visitor had to say about the difficulties Gail had experienced before her son was placed in care.

Different Ways of Reaching a Decision

Procedures for reaching decisions in meetings can remain implicit and it is important that all stakeholders are clear about how decisions are to be reached and judge whether this method reflects legitimate or illegitimate power. As well as deciding on the basis of consensus, a particular stakeholder can have the right or responsibility to take the decision or, alternatively, the majority can decide. The processes of the using of a veto and running out of time can also play a part in reaching a decision.

Having a particular right or responsibility

Certain stakeholders may have a right or particular responsibility to take the decision – for example, the chair or the client. The way this right or responsibility is enacted can vary and may involve the decision being taken after the meeting, having heard what the other stakeholders have to say. As has already been discussed, the formal position in John's review is that the chair makes the decision. It is unlikely that the chair will have direct knowledge of the decision situation and so is dependent on the recommendations, evidence and arguments put forward by others. So even though one person has the formal authority to decide, other stakeholders will usually participate in the decision making. This means that although technically the area manager will decide whether placing John with his mother will form the basis of his care plan, in reality this may reflect other ways of achieving a decision. Chairpersons may decide on the basis of: (i) what they think is best after listening to the arguments; (ii) their estimation of the general feel of the meeting; or (iii) they may be influenced by the views of particular stakeholders who have expertise or hold particular positions or whose views are given more weight than others. For example, the area manager may be convinced by the persuasive arguments of Ellen, given that she is the key worker with the most intimate and up-to-date knowledge of the decision situation.

Due to his young age, it would be inappropriate to place the responsibility of deciding on John, nor would it be his mother's decision alone, being a decision in which agreement between stakeholders is needed in order to ensure that John's best interests are promoted. It is the type of decision that can be taken by family group conferences which involve the extended family deciding what to do after listening to what the professionals have to say (Lupton, 1998). There are also decision situations in social work that involve stakeholders meeting together in which it is for the client alone to decide what to do. In adult services, a meeting may be arranged between carers, relatives, and professional workers, for example, when a crisis is experienced by an older person in caring for themselves and decisions need to be taken about their future care. In theory everybody may agree that at 'the end of the day' it is for the client to decide, but there is a danger that the client is dominated by other stakeholders who have good intentions but overwhelming opinions. There is a tension between the older person having autonomy and the other stakeholders' genuine attempts to inter-vene for the sake of the older person's own welfare (Cicirelli, 1992). This reflects the recurring tension within social work between client autonomy and their need for protection.

Majority view

If consensus is not achieved and a particular stakeholder or group of stakeholders do not have a right or responsibility to take the decision, it is tempting to think in terms of a majority decision. Within social democracies much importance is placed on the majority view, with one extra vote being regarded as enough to secure victory. Taking decisions by the majority view in social work can be problematic and is not usually accepted as appropriate. Firstly, one member, one vote may not be applicable because different stakeholders have different rights and responsibilities. Secondly, minority view holders (particularly after a vote) can experience the acceptance of the majority view as a defeat in what has been framed as a win–lose situation. The consequence of this can be that those holding minority views have little commitment to implement the decision and may even wish to sabotage its implementation. Thirdly, the position of minority opinions is given considerable weight in social work and there is a belief that everybody's agreement needs to be sought even if it may be given with varying degrees of enthusiasm.

Having a veto

As well as the power to decide, there is the power to stop a decision being made. There may be stakeholders whose agreement is essential, giving them a veto to prevent a decision being agreed. This may be because stakeholders are endeavouring to achieve a consensus involving the agreement of all stakeholders or because certain stakeholders' agreement is required because of their power, role or status. A distinction can be made between stakeholders whose agreement is required and those whose agreement can be dispensed with. On the face of it, Gail's new partner is not a particularly powerful figure, but his agreement and support would be necessary if John was to be placed with his mother. If he was less than enthusiastic, there would be concern about the chances of the proposed arrangement being successful. By contrast, the agreement of the paediatrician and health visitor, although desirable, may not be considered essential.

Running out of time

Meetings tend to go through a sequence of discussion and then decision. There will come a point during the meeting when the discussion needs to be called to a halt and a decision taken. While time-limits can be useful in concentrating the mind by signalling when the time for discussion has ended and the time for decision arrived, it can be an issue whether stakeholders are in a position to decide when time runs out. Decisions can be taken at the end of meetings for the wrong reasons when stakeholders are tired and want the meeting to finish. There will be situations when no decision is better than an unsound decision and other situations where putting off the decision may be either dangerous or allow the situation to drift. The relevant question is whether the length of time allowed for discussion has been adequate, with a distinction being drawn between situations in which it would be premature to take the decision because the situation has not been fully discussed and those in which there is reluctance to face the issues involved in making a choice. By the end of the meeting stakeholders attending John's review were able to reach broad agreement about him being placed with his mother, while still subject to the care order and for his name to be reinstated on the child protection register with a joint child care review and child protection review to be held in three months' time. When such a consensus is not achieved and no stakeholder has a right or particular responsibility to take the decision, a balance will need to be struck between gaining reluctant agreement by a process of attrition and abandoning the meeting with the decision left undecided.

CHAPTER SUMMARY AND KEY POINTS

In this chapter it has been argued that stakeholders may need to meet together in order to consult with each other but that issues of power will operate within such meetings. Although there are certain potential benefits of meeting together, these may not be achieved unless active steps are taken to bring about their realisation. Careful attention needs to be given to how decisions are actually taken in the meeting, since silence cannot be taken as agreement and all stakeholders need to be clear who has decision making responsibility in relation to particular decisions.

When stakeholders meet together, the following points need to be considered:

- who needs to meet together;
- the issues of power between stakeholders;
- how the potential benefits of meeting together will be realised;
- how decisions are to be reached within the meeting.

Issues and tensions when stakeholders meet together include:

- the client may feel excluded or find it a negative experience;
- meeting together may reinforce dominant power alliances; and
- the necessary chairing and facilitation skills may not be available.

5

Thought and Emotion in Decision Making

Decision making involves both thinking and feeling about the decision situation, but there is controversy about whether intuitive or analytical thought is more suited to social work decisions and whether emotions have a positive or negative impact on decision making. This chapter explores different ways of thinking and feeling about the decision situation and the factors that may promote and hinder vigilant thought. It is divided into three sections concerned with: two ways of thinking, the impact of emotions and the role of internal conflict.

ILLUSTRATIVE EXAMPLE

Mr Smith is an 81-year-old widower who is in hospital after suffering a stroke and is now ready for discharge. His daughter, Gloria, who lives some distance away, is concerned about him returning home to an empty house. Esther is the hospital social worker. She sees her role as facilitating Mr Smith to make a decision about whether to return home or go into residential care. Part of this facilitation means enabling Mr Smith and his daughter to consider the possible consequences of the two options so that they will be more able to make an informed decision.

Two Ways of Thinking

Esther, Mr Smith and Gloria will be involved in thinking about the decision situation, the term *thinking* being used in a general and somewhat imprecise way to refer to both deliberative and nondeliberative mental processes by which people make sense of situations. There has been rivalry throughout history between two distinct forms of thinking, intuition and analysis (Hammond, 1996, p. 60) and a contrast between the two has been made in various guises in literature influential in social work. England (1986) compares the *intuitive use of self* to *scientific rationality*. Schon (1995) contrasts *knowledge in action* (which is akin to intuition) to *technical rationality* and Dreyfus and Dreyfus (1986, p. 16) refer to the difference between *human intuition* and *calculative rationality*. All these authors give intuition or its equivalent as the favoured alternative, but in rejecting a scientific, technical or calculative approach they are in danger of turning their back on analysis which is not inevitably scientific, technical or calculative. The controversy over the roles of intuition and analysis in social work decision making is related to but should not be confused with the dispute over whether social work is an art or a science. For those interested in the latter dispute see England (1986, chapter 6).

Decision situations in social work are unstructured in the sense that they consist of a potentially unlimited number of elements each impacting on the others in an uncertain way. By the very nature of unstructured situations it is not possible to construct effective technical rules for determining the features of the problem and the best course of action. In such circumstances it is tempting for social work theoreticians to maintain that it is only professional intuition that can be used to make such decisions. At a time when professional intuition is being undermined with the introduction of bureaucratic forms of assessment (Howe, 1992), there is a danger that the argument becomes polarised between intuitive decision making and technical decision making. It needs to be recognised that analysis is not inevitably technical; together with intuition, it provides two equally valuable ways of thinking (R. Adams, 1995, p. 398) that are available to professional workers. Although decision making in social work is neither purely intuitive or purely analytical they will be described separately below.

Intuition

The use of intuition is often seen as an important aspect of professional decision making but its definition and nature are problematic (Hamm, 1988, p. 81). Intuition has been variously described as the absence of analysis (Hammond, 1996, p. 60), the pinnacle of expertise (Dreyfus and Dreyfus, 1986) or the unconscious processing of data (Hamm, 1988, p. 81) but the nature of intuition will be left open, with it being defined by the absence of explicit deliberation. This absence does not mean that intuition is a matter of chance or a guess; rather it means that the basis of the decision is not explicit at the time the decision is made. This process is identified by Baylor as non-analytical reason, 'a special kind of reason that is antithetical to metacognition', which he argues, along with immediacy and formulating connections, form the three components of intuition (Baylor, 1997, p. 188). Many extravagant claims have been made as regards intuition, such as it never being a source of erroneous reasoning (Baylor, 1997, p. 192), but it can be thought of quite modestly as deciding in a relatively holistic way, without breaking down the decision situation into its various elements. In this view intuitive decisions represent a kind of gestalt which retains the wholeness of the complete picture without prior intellectualisation (England, 1986; Braye and Preston-Shoot, 1992, p. 59).

The absence of deliberation means that intuition is a relatively quick way of deciding that can make use of limited information by sensing patterns and filling in gaps. Professional intuition will be regarded as an ability that develops through experience which cannot be formally taught. Some people may be regarded as having more natural capacity than others to make intuitive decisions. To be reliable and accurate, intuition needs to be based on expertise that has been developed over a period of time and although having an important role within professional work, intuitive decision making has a number of drawbacks which stem from its implicit nature. The most important of these shortcomings is that the reasons behind intuitive decisions are not readily available for comment and scrutiny, which is necessary in partnership work. This contrasts with analysis in which the reasoning of the decision maker is explicit and can be directly assessed. Intuition is also used in everyday life where it is based on life experience or more controversially a natural intuitive ability. Gloria believes her father to be at unacceptable risk if he returns home; as she has not deliberated over the different elements of the decision situation, she could be described as using her intuition to assess the level of risk.

Analysis

Hammond defines analysis as 'a step-by-step, conscious, logically defensible process' (Hammond, 1996, p. 60) and it will be regarded here as a process of breaking down the decision situation into a number of elements and carefully considering the elements in relation to each other. Chapter 6 gives a way of analysing the decision situation in terms of key factors, decision goals and a set of options. Chapter 7 gives different ways of analysing options in order to decide what course of action to take. These processes involve a simplification of the decision situation, with conscious deliberation over the different elements in a systematic and orga- nised way. In this way, analysis uses a few chosen aspects of the decision situation in a precise manner. This contrasts sharply with intuition in which there is no conscious attempt to break down the decision task, with framing the information and choice of option taking place implicitly. Analysis can be thought of as using selected information in a precise way, whereas intuition uses all of the perceived information of the decision maker, in an imprecise way. Esther suggests that Mr Smith and Gloria join her in analysing the risks involved in both returning home and going into a residential home. She explains that this would include carefully considering each option in terms of dangers and potential benefits. Although this would take time she believes it would put them in a better position to make an informed decision that they were less likely to regret.

The strength of analysis is that it encourages openness about reasoning and so potentially holds decision making open to scru- tiny. Analysis can make explicit the judgements about uncertainty and value that need to be made within social work and is an approach that can be formally taught and learnt. A judgement will always be needed as to whether the results of analysis will be worth the investment of time. Analysing the decision situation can become so complex that it hinders rather than aids sound decision making. One criticism of analysis concerns the misplaced faith it can induce in the ability to make reliable predictions in fields such as engineer- ing, where in conditions of uncertainty it can result in catastrophes. This has a parallel in the increasing faith placed in risk assessments in social work, where there is a danger that decision makers get so caught up in the detail of the analysis that they become over- confident about the reliability and validity of their information and predictive techniques or beset with indecision because the process makes clear there is no valid basis of making scientific predictions.

Combining intuition and analysis

There is a tendency to polarise approaches into two opposing camps or theoretical positions which can bring clarity and greater understanding, but can also obscure the potential compatibility and complementarity of approaches. Martinez-Brawley and Zorita propose that social work represents a 'very desirable convergence' of art and science (Martinez–Brawley and Zorita, 1998). In a similar vein, social work decision making is a collage (to use their word) of what here has been referred to as intuition and analysis. Some decisions in social work will need breaking down into their component parts and given careful consideration but because social work decision making involves issues of uncertainty and value, intuition needs to be used within analysis to make judgements about the significance of information. As will be seen in Chapter 7, professional intuition plays an important role within analysis in the making of judgements about the likelihood and value of possible outcomes. Combining the explicitness of analysis with the skilled judgements of professional intuition means that purely intuitive decision making can be improved by making use of analysis and analysis is still possible even when the component decisions are a matter of professional judgement.

Social workers need to know how to go about analysis, while at the same time developing their intuitive expertise, as both intuition and analysis have important roles within social work. When experienced and skilled social workers need to make decisions relatively quickly, intuition is most likely to be the best approach. When there is more time to make a decision, they can make a judgement as to whether an analytical approach is indicated, which will tend to be when the potential consequences of the decision justify the investment of time. This is most likely to be in risky, complex or unfamiliar decision situations. Practice teachers are likely to use analysis when explaining to their students how to approach a particular decision, even if it is a decision they would have taken intuitively. When facilitating client decision making or making decisions in partnership, some degree of analysis will be needed as these approaches involve being explicit about the basis of choice.

FIGURE 5.1   *The use of intuition and analysis in social work*

	beginner worker	skilled worker
intuition	only when the necessary knowledge and skill have been developed through experience	day-to-day practice
analysis	day-to-day practice	difficult or unfamiliar decision situations (when there is time), when teaching students, working in partnership or facilitating client decision making

Inexperienced social workers will need to take a more analytical approach to decision making because they will not have developed the necessary expertise. There is a danger that they will use their intuition despite their lack of relevant experience, as it tends to be the default thought process used in the absence of an alternative. Where there is no time for an analytical approach, beginning social workers need to seek the guidance of more experienced workers. Figure 5.1 summarises the different uses of intuition and analysis in social work.

Substantive thinkers or 'cognitive misers'

Another way of contrasting thinking styles is between substantive thought and the use of heuristics. Many of the findings of social psychological research indicate that people don't think in a substantive way when asked to estimate probabilities in the experimental laboratory (Kahneman, Stovic and Tversky, 1982). Instead they use what are called heuristics, in the sense of taking short cuts in thinking, to make up their mind. The use of the term heuristics in this context should not be confused with its use in the philosophy of science, where it refers to methods concerned with discovery as opposed to verification. These short cuts or rules of thumb are efficient in terms of the mental energy used and in many situations can form the basis of sound decisions but can also give rise to errors due to a built-in bias (see Strachan, 1997). Although decision experiments carried out in a laboratory are open to a number of criticisms, they do show that under certain circumstances people use heuristics to crudely simplify decision tasks rather than systematically and deliberatively thinking about them. This research led to a view of people as cognitive misers (Tetlock, 1985) using as little mental energy as possible when it came to decision making. In recognition that the decision tasks given to people in social psychological experiments are of necessity out of context, a more balanced view is needed, with people being seen as having different ways of approaching decision making, depending on their perception of the decision task and the context (Tetlock, 1985). With some tasks and in some contexts, short cuts will be used, while in others substantive processing will take place (Forgas, 1995, p.40).

The availability heuristic

The availability heuristic is an example of one of these short cuts to making judgements and decisions (Kahneman, Stovic and Tversky, 1982). This heuristic involves a person's estimate of the likelihood of an event happening being based on how available that event is in their memory, which can relate to various factors including recent experience of the event, the frequency of its occurrence and the salience and vividness of the event. Although many older people fear being victims of crime if they leave their homes, this is not based on the actual statistical risk (which is quite low). Media reports of such crimes and the vividness of the television images of bruised victims may have increased the availability of such events in older people's memories. A similar explanation could be given for Gloria's extreme worry about her father falling and being unable to summon help. She believes it is very likely that if her father returns home, he will fall and be unable to summon help. If Gloria was using the availability heuristic, her estimate of risk would depend on the high availability in her memory of the event of falling and being unable to summon help.

She has heard many stories recently about such things happening, as well as reports in the media of people dying in their homes and being undiscovered for weeks. The vividness, traumatic nature and salience for her of the event is likely to increase its availability in her memory. As well as overestimates of an event occurring, the availability heuristic can lead to underestimates when events are not readily available in the memory. The availability heuristic can give a reasonable estimate, but more often it will have little relation to the actual risk which is seen as depending more on baseline information about the number of people who live alone after being discharged home in her father's condition and the proportion of this total who experience a fall and are unable to summon help. This baseline information is regarded as forming a more appropriate basis for estimating likelihood than the availability heuristic but is often not available for the types of decision situations encountered in social work.

Because intuition is based on experience, the question can arise as to whether the term intuition is another way of describing the use of heuristics. There have been attempts to apply knowledge for heuristics to professional intuition (Cioffi, 1997) but within the decision making literature the term 'heuristics' is so associated with built-in bias, that it may need to be reserved for inappropriate short cuts. Although intuition may involve the use of heuristics, in the sense that it is a short cut in thinking, the important issue is how valid the basis of a particular intuition is. Gloria's intuition about her father may be based on sound knowledge gained over the years or could be based on something like the potentially erroneous availability heuristic. If Esther was to use her professional intuition to estimate the risk Mr Smith was exposed to, if he returned home, she would be using her professional expertise developed through experience. At least part of this expertise would relate to her experience of people in Mr Smith's circumstances being discharged home and what subsequently happened to them. Intuition may be characterised as a short cut by its opponents but the acid test is whether it represents the use of skill and sound knowledge or a quick, often erroneous, substitute for substantive processing of information.

The Impact of Emotions

Decision making is most often associated with thinking, with the emotions being seen as irrelevant factors that need to be excluded. However, decision makers not only need to think about the decision situation, they need to be aware of the emotions they experience and the impact they are having. Although emotions are integral to decision situations, there can be ambivalence about their place within social work, with sensitivity to emotion being both an essential quality and a source of danger. Both too little and too much emotion can be regarded as a bad thing; while a particular emotion in one context is considered appropriate, in another it can be regarded as inappropriate. The absence of emotion in a particular situation can be seen as inhuman, while at the same time it is easy to imagine how a person, whether client or social worker, can be overwhelmed by emotion.

What is an emotion?

It is not easy to define what an emotion is, there being different perspectives on emotions. Emotions will be regarded as resulting from an individual's personal appraisal of the situation he or she faces. For example, if the appraisal is one of threat, loss or achievement it will evoke the corresponding emotion, for example, fear, unhappiness or pride (Lazarus, 1991). An emotion, being the result of a person's appraisal of the situation, indicates what the person's assessment of the situation is. So rather than being opposed to thinking, emotions are a product of thinking processes. This means that thinking and emotion are not diametrically opposed to each other as is often thought but rather inextricably linked to each other. There are hundreds of words in the English language denoting different emotions – some are pleasant, like joy and elation, while others are unpleasant, like anxiety and guilt, and still others are more ambiguous like hope, relief, gratitude and compassion. The limitation of space has meant that the unpleasant emotions have been given a greater share of the attention but it needs to be remembered that the more pleasant emotions have an equal place in social work.

Social work and emotions

Emotions are an integral part of social work that need to be acknowledged, understood and worked with. Social workers need to sustain 'an appropriate professional role when deep emotions are involved and when ambivalence and conflict are integral to the situations within which social workers . . . must work' (Stevenson, 1986, p. 505). A wide range of emotions are experienced in social work – such as fear, anxiety, hope and compassion. Furthermore, social workers have to cope with not only their own emotions, but also those of clients and other stakeholders. During an interview Esther experiences fear when Mr Smith waves his stick at her. She feels anger when she learns that a client who moved to residential care has been sexually abused by a member of staff. She feels a sense of loss and sadness when a client dies while awaiting discharge from hospital. She feels happiness when a client finds the strength to oppose the medical staff and fulfils the wish to return home despite the risks.

The impact of emotions on thinking

People in the grip of high emotions are often accused of not thinking straight, but emotions can promote vigilant thinking as well as undermine it. In fact emotions can impact on thinking and thought in a number of ways (Oatley and Jenkins, 1996, p. 102) with individual emotions either having a positive or negative influence on achieving the decision makers' goals. The experience of an emotion can change priorities – either appropriately or inappropriately, distort thinking or provide the motivation to think carefully about the decision situation. Fear can mean that a particular aspect of the decision situation can come to dominate at the expense of others, with an overwhelming desire to escape the object of the fear. Judgement can be clouded by the compassion felt for a client and the overwhelming urge to help. Anxiety can affect the ability to think clearly as it is hard to stop worrying about what is going to happen and anger can disrupt concentration as thoughts turn to how to get one's own back. Emotions can also provide the motivation to put energy into achieving decision goals – for example, pride in a job well done can fuel the pursuit of further success.

Emotions originating outside the decision situation

An important distinction is between those emotions that are an integral part of the decision situation (with each stakeholder having their own emotional response) and emotions which have their origins outside the decision situation. Mr Smith is the client and is at the centre of the decision situation. His emotions need to be regarded as integral to it and so part of a holistic assessment. Gloria, although an important stakeholder, does not have the same central position. There may be events in her life, independent of her relationship with her father, that may have triggered emotions that spill over and impact on her thinking about her father's situation. For example, unbeknown to her father and Esther, Gloria could have anxieties about her own health that spill over to her thinking about her father's situation. She may displace some of her uncertainty about her own future onto her fears about her father's future.

Professional workers may endeavour to keep their personal lives and their professional lives separate. For most of the time they may manage to do so, but there may be occasions when separation becomes impossible and they spill over in either direction. The impact of this spill-over in the direction of home-to-work is a neglected area (Crouter, 1984, p. 426). Esther may have less mental energy to give to her job having experienced a loss in her personal life, which may impact on her thinking about Mr Smith and his situation. The work/personal-life boundary is not the only one that social workers endeavour to maintain. There is also the boundary between the different cases that make up a social worker's workload and the boundaries between work with clients and the emotions involved in being located in an organisation.

Emotions originating within the decision situation

The social worker, clients and other stakeholders will experience emotions evoked by the decision situation. Gloria is feeling anxious about her father returning home, but uncertain about how he would settle in residential care. The fear of him returning home is pushing her towards residential care as a solution and she wants to put an end to the uncertainty quickly. As a consequence she doesn't want to take the time to analyse the decision situation and puts pressure on Esther by continually ringing her up asking when her father is moving into a home. She makes negative comments on Esther's competence and asks her whether she knows what she is doing. This provokes an emotional reaction within Esther. She feels anger towards Gloria and sorry for Mr Smith, who she believes to be dominated by his daughter.

Coping with emotions

There are a number of different aspects of emotions that need to be coped with. Three will be distinguished here: the physiological reaction, the expression or display of emotion and the action tendency (Lazarus, 1991). People may not have much control over the initial arousal of an emotion (which is prompted by the personal meaning the situation has for them) including their bodies' physiological reactions, but people can control how they display and act upon the emotions once aroused. The display of an emotion has less direct impact on decision making than the action tendency triggered, nevertheless it is an important consideration. Within occupations and organisations there are explicit and implicit feeling rules that govern what can and what cannot be expressed and when (Fineman, 1995, p. 127). It would be regarded as inappropriate for Esther as a professional social worker to let her anger show in her tone of voice while she is speaking to Gloria. It may be permissible to show it to her colleagues and team manager, depending on the organisational and team culture. The management of the expression of feelings, being polite when you feel like being rude, is one of the many sources of stress for people working in service industries (Fineman, 1995, p. 129).

More important in relation to decision making is the action tendency of an emotion. Lazarus identifies this as one of the defining features of an emotion (Lazarus, 1991, p. 87). An emotion can trigger a certain tendency to do something, with each individual emotion having its own characteristic action tendency. If people perceive themselves as having been demeaned, they experience anger and the action tendency is to retaliate. If a person feels compassion, the action tendency is to reach out and help. The action tendencies of emotions can have significant impact on thinking about decision situations and need to be appropriately managed. Esther is feeling angry with Gloria and wants to tell her a few 'home truths'. She has compassion towards Mr Smith who, she believes, doesn't know which way to turn and feels like rescuing him from his domineering daughter.

Action tendencies, although having some potential to be a positive influence in the decision situation, generally only make matters worse if they are acted upon in an ill-considered way. Verbally attacking Gloria would be considered unprofessional and attempting to rescue Mr Smith and in effect take the place of Gloria would be counter-productive and make matters worse. Esther manages to control her emotions by holding on to her anger until she finishes the telephone conversation with Gloria and then discusses Gloria's attitude with a colleague. There are a number of other ways social workers could cope with their emotions and their action tendencies. As stated above, an emotion depends on the personal appraisal of the situation by the person concerned and an important way of coping with negative emotions is to reappraise the personal meaning of the situation. Esther initially feels Gloria is demeaning her with her comments and feels angry but on reflection she reappraises the situation as Gloria being worried about her father and ceases to feel anger. Another way social workers protect themselves from pain and survive their harrowing work (Satyamurti, 1981) is to distance themselves from the decision situation and the people within it. An appropriate professional distance involves not being too involved or too distant. Of course, maintaining such a balance is not straightforward and can be a source of tension and conflict. Less appropriate ways of managing emotion are to avoid considering the aspect of the decision situation that evokes the emotion or to deny that the emotion is being felt.

Stress and thinking

Stress can be defined in a number of different ways, with there being a distinction between the subjective experience of stress and the external demands on a person. Lazarus and Lazarus (1994) define stress as occurring when there is a subjective imbalance between the perceived demands made on a person and their perceived resources to manage these demands. Pressure is necessary to mobilise the intellectual, emotional, social and physical resources necessary to make sound decisions; but pressure of too great an intensity, over too long a period has a detrimental effect. Social work is regarded as a stressful job, with demands tending to exceed the resources to manage them. This has been the source of some concern (Gibson, McGrath and Reid, 1989; Jones, Fletcher and Ibbetson, 1991), but comparatively little attention has been paid to the impact of stress on the decision makers' ability to think about the decision situation. Specific and non-specific stress can be seen as potentially having different kinds of impact on thinking. A specific stress emanating from the demands of the decision situation is more likely to motivate vigilant thinking, while stress from one's workload in general is more likely to impair thinking. Continual working under stress can result in the burnout that is associated with emotional exhaustion, depersonalisation and lack of personal accomplishment. Social workers experiencing burnout may avoid thinking about and getting involved in difficult situations (see McGee, 1989).

Individuals have different capacities for coping with varying levels of pressure; with what motivates one person, being the source of breakdown of another. Esther is feeling generally under pressure and harassed by her workload and Gloria is a source of further pressure. It could be that this pressure is the last straw and Esther goes off sick or it motivates her to put even more energy into thinking through the decision situation with the stakeholders. A number of factors are thought to strengthen the capacity to cope with pressure – including support from colleagues, management and social networks outside work. Other significant factors in coping with pressure are thought to be clarity of role, control over work, high organisational morale, good professional supervision, a clear work/personal-life boundary and the ability to relax away from work (Thompson *et al.*, 1994, p. 163).

Janis and Mann's Conflict Theory

Even though high emotions can be impediments to clear thinking, they may also be necessary to provide the motivation to invest in sound decision making. In their conflict theory of decision making, Janis and Mann (1977) identify internal conflict, hope and time as requirements for, what they term, vigilant information processing. The origin of the theory is in research into people's responses to warnings of imminent disasters, like a flood, but it has much wider applicability and gives insight into decision making under stress, thereby connecting the two areas of thought and emotion. The vigilant information processing that Janis and Mann have in mind relates more to analysis than intuition, involving as it does deliberation.

At the backbone of their theory are four basic questions:

- Are the risks serious if I *don't* change?
- Are the risks serious if I *do* change?
- Is it realistic to hope to find a better solution?
- Is there sufficient time to search and deliberate?

If the answer to all four questions is *yes,* vigilant information processing is possible. In their original research this would have taken the form of believing, in the context of receiving a flood warning, that it was risky to stay put and risky to evacuate, while at the same time believing there was time to think in the hope of

FIGURE 5.2   *Janis and Mann's four basic questions*

Are the risks serious if I *don't* change? If no, stay the same (unconflicted adherence)	If yes, go to next question
Are the risks serious if I *do* change? If no, change (unconflicted change)	If yes, *conflict*
Is it realistic to hope to find a better solution? If no, procrastinate, pass the buck or bolster (defensive avoidance)	If yes, *hope*
Is there sufficient time to search and deliberate? If no, panic (hyper vigilance)	If yes, *time*

finding a solution. How the four questions give rise to the three ingredients of internal conflict, hope and time is shown in figure 5.2.

Lack of internal conflict

Within Janis and Mann's theory, the lack of internal conflict leads to either unconflicted adherence or unconflicted change – both of which are impaired coping strategies. Gloria is clear that her father will be at severe risk if he returns home, so for her the risks are serious if her father doesn't change his living situation. Consequently, her answer to the first question is *yes*. If this had not been the case, with her believing that her father could return home without serious risk, this would have been an example of *unconflicted adherence*, a coping strategy based on the belief that there is no serious risk involved in not changing. Gloria believes there are no risks involved in her father moving to residential care, so her answer to the second question is *no*, the risks are *not* serious if her father changes. This means that she has no internal conflict and she is prepared to engage in *unconflicted change* without the need to vigilantly process the information. If she was to change her mind about the risks involved in her father moving to residential care, she would start to experience internal conflict and so need to think carefully about what to do.

Lack of hope

Mr Smith is experiencing internal conflict. He believes there are serious risks involved both if he returns home and if he moves to residential care. So his answers to the first two questions are *yes*. At the present time he does not see an alternative to being unhappy either by giving up his home or going back home to live alone and being a worry to Gloria. So his answer to the third question is *no,* he does not believe it is realistic to hope for a better solution. In this context, hope needs to be distinguished from optimism. Hope is 'an antidote to despair . . . one hopes a bad situation will improve' (Lazarus and Lazarus, 1994, p. 73), while optimism involves a positive expectation. To be hopeful is to see some sense in striving to overcome obstacles and in the absence of hope Mr Smith is reluctant to consider his options and engages in what Janis and Mann refer to as defensive avoidance. They identify three strategies used to avoid processing the information vigilantly despite the presence of internal conflict.

The first is *procrastination*, which happens when the risks are perceived as not serious if the decision is postponed. As there is pressure to free Mr Smith's bed, the decision cannot be postponed for long and so it is too risky to delay the decision. The next strategy is *buck-passing* and is available if there is somebody else to turn the decision making over to. However, since Esther, Gloria and the medical staff are all clear that it is his decision, Mr Smith can only fall back on the last strategy, that of *bolstering,* which involves him choosing the least objectionable alternative and bolstering it. That is, he exaggerates the good points and ignores the disadvantages of the least objectionable course of action and so avoids systematically examining the options. For Mr Smith, the least objectionable alternative is moving to residential care and so he minimises the losses involved in giving up his home and emphasises the advantages of residential care. The role of hope in decision making is an important but neglected area that affects both clients and social workers, who can develop a cynical attitude as a response to the contradictory pressures and the lack of resources. The impact of a lack of hope that things can improve needs to be contrasted with the dangers of false hope that were discussed in Chapter 3 in the context of involving the client. Janis and Mann's conflict theory points to the need for hope if information is to be processed vigilantly.

Lack of time

Esther experiences internal conflict because she considers there are serious risks in both Mr Smith's premature discharge and in continuing to withstand the pressure from the consultant to free the bed. Her experience and professional education have given her hope that there is a better solution, leaving the question for her as whether there is *time* to work with Mr Smith and Gloria to facilitate the vigilant processing of information. If she perceives there is time, then she has all the ingredients for vigilant information processing to take place. If she doesn't perceive there to be time, she will move into what Janis and Mann refer to as hyper vigilance, which is something akin to panic. Vigilant information processing will not of course be enough to bring about a good outcome, but it is necessary

FIGURE 5.3 *Four types of impaired information processing*

---

1 Unconflicted Adherence
(the risks of doing nothing are **not** serious so do nothing)

2 Unconflicted Change
(the risks of change are **not serious, so change**)

3 Defensive Avoidance
(there is **no hope of finding a better solution**)

    (i)   Procrastinating
           (the risks are **not serious if the decision is postponed**)

    (ii)   Buck-Passing
           (the decision can be turned over to someone else)

    (iii) Bolstering
           (the risks are serious if the decision is postponed, it canot be turned over to someone else, so pick the least objectionable option and bolster it) .

4 Hyper Vigilance (panic)
(there is **not** sufficient time to think about the decision)

in order to engage in systematic appraisal of the options. Figure 5.3 summarises how Janis and Mann's theory gives rise to four types of impaired information processing.

It would be a mistake to overextend the application of this theory to social work situations, but it does give insights into the impediments to people engaging in explicit consideration of the options. It is particularly useful, as the above example demonstrates, in pinpointing these impediments and so enabling them to be overcome. Gloria could be worked with to enable her to see that residential care isn't a completely straightforward risk-free solution, Mr Smith needs to gain hope that a satisfactory solution can be found and Esther needs to gain time so that she can work with Mr Smith and Gloria to enable them to systematically consider the options.

CHAPTER SUMMARY AND KEY POINTS

This chapter has considered thinking processes and emotions in relation to decision making in social work. Intuition and analysis were identified as different ways of thinking, but rather than them being mutually exclusive they can (and within social work need to be) used alongside each other. Intuition needs to have a sound basis if it is not to degenerate into a heuristic device that crudely simplifies complex decision situations, while analysis often needs its component decisions to be based on professional intuition. The systematic processing of thought can be prevented or interfered with in a number of ways. Emotions such as fear can have a potential negative impact, but internal conflict may be necessary to provide motivation to expend mental energy on systematically considering the options. Nevertheless in the absence of hope and time, internal conflict may lead to defensive avoidance or panic.

When thinking and feeling about decision situations, stakeholders need to:

- consider whether the decision requires analysis;
- check they are not taking inappropriate short cuts in their thinking;
- be aware of the emotions involved and the impact they are having.

Issues and tensions when thinking and feeling about decision situations include:

- whether there is time to carry out a full analysis;
- whether any intuitions used have a sound basis; and
- being sensitive to the emotions involved but not letting them inappropriately impact on thinking.

6

Framing the Decision Situation

When making a choice, decision makers have a mental image or frame of the decision situation, constructed through the selection, interpretation and organisation of information. The process of constructing decision frames in social work needs to be explicit, purposeful and free from bias, as the soundness of a decision depends on whether the frame reflects a full range of factors without the distorting effects of unfounded beliefs. The structuring of an otherwise random array of information requires the active involvement of clients and other stakeholders and will be considered to have three components: a picture of the situation, decision goals and a set of options. Decision framing and professional social work assessment both aim to develop an understanding of the client's situation. Although having many issues in common, decision framing specifically focuses on the decision situation and is not restricted to a preliminary stage of the social work process as assessment sometimes is.

ILLUSTRATIVE EXAMPLE

Winston and Alice are both in their late seventies, with Alice being in the middle stages of dementia. She has started to wander and her husband has taken to locking the front and back doors of the house so that she cannot get out. Bill, a social worker in the adults' team, is the care manager and the couple have home assistance five days a week. The home help has reported back to Bill that Winston is getting increasingly exasperated. Last week the home help found him trying to physically restrain Alice and she now feels something must be done. Bill decides to arrange a conference between the different stakeholders, which include: Alice, Winston, the home help, Bill, the family GP and Preston (Alice and Winston's only son). Together they will construct a frame of the decision situation in order to determine what to do if anything.

A Picture of the Situation

A picture of the situation can be likened to a mosaic made up of pieces of information arranged in a particular way to produce an understanding of the decision situation. Who actually constructs the picture will depend on the client's level of involvement (see Chapter 3): the social worker may facilitate the client's decision framing; or the client and social worker may endeavour to negotiate a joint picture; or the social worker may consult the client on what should be included. The decision frame can also be co-constructed by the stakeholders meeting together, as will be the case in Alice and Winston's situation.

Holistic perspective

Social workers endeavour to construct holistic pictures that reflect the complexity of decision situations but are often constrained by their agencies to narrow the focus by the introduction of tick box assessment (Sheppard, 1995b, p. 276). A holistic perspective attempts to encompass the whole picture taking into account a wide range of factors on a number of interconnected levels including the personal, interpersonal, environmental and sociocultural levels. Clients are respected as unique individuals, with their own feelings, beliefs and aspirations, who interact with significant others, within complex interlocking social contexts. The ability to deal with complexity is identified by Fook, Ryan and Hawkins (1997) as a distinctive feature of social work expertise, the aim being to do justice to the interconnections of people's lives including their past, present situation and future possibilities. Even though the picture may be complex, it will remain a simplification of a much more complex social reality and can never be regarded as complete and definitive. Despite this, there has been a trend for assessment (and so decision frames) to become mechanistic, routinised and technical, being based on a bureaucratic model rather than a professional one (Howe, 1992; Lloyd and Taylor, 1995). This means assessments can fail to provide an appropriate basis for decisions. The picture that is constructed of the decision situation needs to reflect social work's distinctive perspective which stresses the multifaceted nature of situations, their context and the uniqueness of the client – although this may not always be achieved in practice. Dorothy Scott found in her study of social work assessment in cases of alleged child abuse that a proceduralised model of practice was often followed 'which narrowed the range of factors considered' (Scott, 1998, p. 73).

Building a picture

An adaptation of Brunswik's lens model of judgement is one way of thinking about how the decision frame is produced. The psychologist Egon Brunswik likened the process by which several factors are combined together to form a mental representation of the environment, to the way a camera lens collects light together to form an image on film (Leeper, 1966, p. 415). Brunswik thereby viewed judgement in terms of the relationship between the real environmental system and the decision maker's mental representation of that system (Hogarth, 1987, p. 8). A decision maker builds up an integrated mental representation of the decision situation by combining together a number of relevant factors as shown in Figure 6.1. These factors are 'fallible' (Hammond, 1996, p. 87) in the sense that they only indicate rather than provide evidence of what is happening and so can lead to mistaken inferences. A distinction can be made between tangible and intangible factors: those that can be perceived through the senses and those that cannot. Hammond places emphasis on the tangible nature of factors (also known as

FIGURE 6.1 *How factors are used to construct a mental picture of the decision situation*

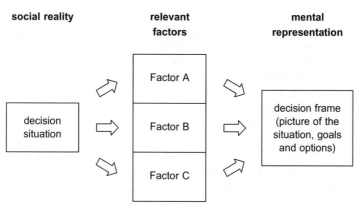

Source: Adapted from Hogarth, 1990, p. 9.

cues or indicators) that are available to make inferences about the intangible (Hammond, 1996, p. 87) but social work decision frames need to include a wide range of factors, some of which will be less tangible than others. Examples of some of the more tangible factors identified by Bill are: the locking of the front and back doors so Alice cannot go out; Alice's apparently aimless searching around the house; and her distressed husband following her in a vain attempt to get her to sit down. Although such a model can be helpful, it should not be taken literally or used beyond its usefulness.

Identifying the pieces

Identifying relevant factors to be taken into account, and giving these appropriate meaning and weight, are key skills in building a picture of the decision situation. A flawed or partial picture will mean an unsound decision, but the process of identifying the pieces of the picture is problematic as it involves sifting through the information and giving it significance. A focus on processes of need, harm or life problems can mean the picture being skewed to the negative side of people's lives and care is needed to include the client's resources, strengths and life satisfactions. Perception is of necessity selective, there being far more information potentially available in the environment than can be processed. This means that decision framing involves a series of micro decisions about what information is selected and what meaning it is given. These micro decisions are shaped by what the decision maker believes to be important (their values), their models of how the social universe works (their social understandings or theories) and how they are feeling (their motivation). Space does not permit a full discussion of the problematic nature of the knowledge base used to make decision frames in social work but see Sheppard (1995a) for discussion of the issues in relation to assessments.

As decision situations consist of a potentially vast number of factors, there are constraints in obtaining a full picture. Some of these constraints are inevitable given the limits on time and the human capacity to process information, some are contingent on the amount of accessible information obtainable in a particular situation, while others are imposed on professional social work by its agency context. Already noted has been the trend to proceduralise and so control the assessment process, often with the aim of narrowing its focus. There may also be a lack of knowledge about what are the potentially relevant and important factors to attend to. Social workers need to develop knowledge about life and life issues (Sibeon, 1990, p. 34), so as to be able to appreciate the significance of particular factors, and avoid what Minty (1995, p. 50) refers to as 'social work's marked tendency to become preoccupied with single issues to the exclusion of other relevant considerations'. Social workers also need the interpersonal skills necessary to communicate with people and enable them to tell their own story. As Alice's verbal communications are not readily understandable, there is a danger that how she feels will be ignored. How she is feeling is likely to be expressed through her non-verbal communication, including her facial expression and posture (O'Sullivan, 1990), but could easily be missed and so not taken into account in the construction of the decision frame.

Putting the pieces together

The process of putting the pieces back together in a 'creative synthesis' (Imbrogno and Canada, 1988, p. 21) is problematic and there can be ambiguity about what sense to make of the picture. For example, does Winston's handling of Alice constitute abuse? The minds of decision makers can become predisposed to seeing the decision situation in a particular way, as when the Orkney inquiry found that the minds of the managers considering the removal of a number of children from their families were predisposed towards seeing allegations of ritual abuse as reliable (Clyde, 1992, p. 229). Notwithstanding the problematic nature of factors and how they fit together, they need to be placed in relation to each other to form a coherent integrated picture. At the very least, the key factors need to be listed to form a summary of the decision makers' understanding of the situation. The stakeholders' list of key factors in Alice and Winston's situation included:

- The home help is distressed by both Alice's wandering and Winston's attempts to settle her. Of all the stakeholders that live outside the household, she has the most detailed knowledge of what is happening in the decision situation.
- Alice does not give coherent answers to questions and so it is not possible to ascertain her wishes directly, but she does not appear from her non-verbal communication to be distressed or agitated.

- The substituted judgement (see Chapter 3) that has been constructed in respect of Alice is that she wishes to remain in her own home with her husband.
- In the long term Alice's dementia will worsen.
- Alice is being effectively confined to the house, but it is unclear whether this can regarded as a form as abuse or justified as a caring activity given Alice's state of mind.
- Winston, although in good health, is very distressed and exasperated by his wife's behaviour.
- Winston wants to remain with his wife in their own home and believes that she wants to stay with him.
- Although Winston does not welcome Bill and the home help's involvement, he has not refused them access to the house.
- Preston only takes a peripheral role in relation to his parents' situation but believes his mother would be better off in residential care.
- There is no known history of violence between the couple. The GP has found slight bruising on Alice's arms, but is unsure whether this results from Winston holding her or her bumping into things.
- Most of the stakeholders in the situation are committed to Alice staying in her own home, as long as she or her husband do not experience unacceptable levels of distress or harm.

Bill is very mindful of the danger of ignoring or denying that some form of abuse is occurring in domestic settings involving older people (Penhale, 1993, p. 100) and that Alice's age, gender and dementia make her vulnerable to abuse (Aitken and Griffin, 1996, p. 123). Nevertheless the picture that emerged from the meeting was of a difficult situation that did not warrant being regarded as abuse, but one in need of continuing support and monitoring.

The nature of the pieces

Objective reality can be regarded as what is actually the case in a situation, but the notion of reality is highly problematic and needs to be used with caution (Spinelli, 1989). At least three perspectives can be identified as to the nature of the pieces of information that fit together to form a picture of the situation. In a *pieces as facts* view, an objective reality exists and human beings potentially have access to it. Within a *pieces as interpretations* view, an objective reality may exist but human beings have no direct access, it being something that is only open to interpretation based on individual and collective experience. In a *pieces as social constructions* view, there is no culturally free objective reality with human beings' sense of reality being socially constructed and the belief in an unconstructed reality being unfounded. The three views have their strengths and weaknesses, and a picture of the situation can be regarded as potentially a mixture of facts, interpretations and social constructions.

Facts

In the *pieces as facts* view, decision makers endeavour to be 'objective' rather than 'subjective' in their framing of the decision situation, with objectivity being considered possible and subjectivity as something to be avoided. The existence of a culturally free objective reality to which human beings have access is not questioned, with a clear distinction being made between factual information and opinion. Facts are the truth and defined on the basis of evidence – for example, the slight bruising on Alice's arms. Opinions are allowed for but need to be clearly understood as judgements about what is true. The strength of this approach is the emphasis on empirically verifiable evidence that guards against spurious inferences, but its weakness is that pictures of decision situations that consist of just 'facts' are reduced to what has been observed whereas important aspects of decision situations are not open to direct observation. A factual approach to a picture of the situation contrasts with Meyer's view that social work is concerned with creating 'a kind of coherence out of however the client relates his or her story' to give a 'narrative truth' (Meyer, 1993, p. 44).

Interpretations

In the *pieces as interpretations* view, there may be a social reality but human beings have no direct access to it and the best they can hope for is a valid interpretation based on inferences from what is experienced. Meyer (1993, p. 55) regards inference as one of the definitive professional tasks of social workers, with alternative interpretations always being possible. Within this view reality is only accessed through the human senses, which by their very nature are selective and interpretative, with perceived information being imbued with meaning. Subjectivity is regarded as inevitable, but a distinction can be drawn between sound and erroneous interpretations. Whether Alice is being abused or not would be a matter of inference, with what makes an inference valid as opposed to invalid being controversial. The criteria may include the degree to which information is obtained from direct experiences within the situation, as opposed to being imported into or imposed onto the situation as in prejudging, the use of stereotypes and the existence of bias. The strength of the interpretation view is its recognition of the inferential basis of human judgement and its emphasis on the need for inferences to be made on a valid basis but as a number of interpretations are always possible it can lead to indecision.

Social constructions

Within the *social constructionist* view, decision framing is an active process in which the mental picture is socially constructed and is more a cultural story, than a mental representation of a social reality whether directly known or interpreted. The raw materials of this construction are found in the reservoir of cultural meanings available to the decision makers. Social reality is a cultural product, something that human beings have developed, more or less, a consensus about within a particular cultural context (Berger and Luckmann, 1966). Through 'negotiated intelligibility' (Gergen, 1985) certain actions and experiences can become accepted as true, so Alice being regarded as a victim of abuse would be recognised as part of a cultural story that had been given current validity. This view of the picture emphasises the power of those who are in positions 'to determine how situations are to be understood and what knowledge is to count as relevant' (Howe, 1994, p. 526). A social constructionist approach makes all frames of a decision situation problematic and emphasises the possibilities of reframing. Within this perspective all decision frames are provisional, which is an advantage from the point of view of being open to review, but can appear to trivialise such grave matters as abuse with the danger that the approach descends into extreme relativism.

No matter how a picture of the situation is regarded, putting the pieces together is not a once and for all event, but a process in which the picture is under continual review and development. Decision makers may at first have a relatively open mind about the nature of the decision situation. Once this becomes structured through the framing process, there is a danger of their minds becoming closed to the reception of any new information or perspectives that contradict their initial frame. Decision framing needs to be iterative, a term used by Thompson (1996, p. 173) when discussing the assessment process, which means that it needs to be a cyclic process continually striving to improve the understanding of the nature of the decision situation and the processes operating. It would be easy for Bill to either decide that Alice was in no danger or that she was being abused by her husband. It is more difficult to allow for the ambiguity of social situations and keep the decision frame open, with both being seen as possibilities until the picture becomes clearer.

Decision Goals

The second element of the decision frame to be considered is decision goals which are developed from a picture of the situation and the concerns or aspirations of the decision makers. Decision goals will be defined as desired outcomes in relation to the client's own life situation and well-being. They have a strong influence on later stages of decision making, the appraisal of options (Chapter 7) and the evaluation of the outcome of the decision (Chapter 8). Inexperienced social workers may think of goals in terms of providing services or interventions rather than what these are intended to achieve. When developing decision goals they need to be able to identify what is hoped to be achieved rather than the means of achieving it. Part of purposeful professional work is being clear and explicit about goals, but the various stakeholders potentially have different goals and the degree to which they are jointly negotiated will depend on the level of involvement (see Chapter 3). An aim of social work is to frame goals in such a way that they have the widest possibility of being accepted by all stakeholders, but it is not usual in social work for decision making to proceed with a recognition that stakeholders have different goals. A distinction can be made between shorter-term goals and longer-term goals, with a potential tension existing between immediate concerns and long-term planning.

Shorter-term goals

The explicit recognition of shorter-term goals can guard against short-termism, which involves being preoccupied by the immediacy of the situation and losing sight of longer-term concerns. Shorter-term goals can be identified by asking 'What are our immediate concerns?' Bill, the home help and Preston identify the short-term decision making goal as to ease the stress that Winston is under. Winston's short-term goal is to stop what be believes to be interference in his life by his son and the authorities. Short-term goals can be consistent with longer-term goals, but their achievement does not necessarily mean the longer-term goals will be met. For example, social workers and researchers in child care can become, for understandable reasons, fixated with children having a placement and lose sight of the long-term goal of children's overall development (Parker *et al.*, 1991, p. 5). The reverse can also happen when long-term goals are allowed to drive out more immediate goals that can be 'worthy enterprises' in their own right (Sinclair, 1988, p. 112).

Longer-term goals

Longer-term goals tend to relate to people's aspirations for human development, quality of life and states of well-being. They can be lost sight of in the immediacy of the situation. To make sure that any conflicts between shorter- and longer-term goals are not neglected, decision makers will need to explicitly identify both types of goal. Longer-term goals can be identified by asking the question, 'How do we want the outcome of our decision making to be judged?' This question gives the decision makers an appropriate time perspective to consider their longer-term goals and starts them thinking about desirable outcomes. All those at the meeting agreed that the longer-term goals were for both Alice and Winston to have an acceptable quality of life, and for Winston to fulfil his wish to care for his wife as long as this remains compatible with her welfare. There is potentially a conflict between different goals, with the possibility of the shorter-term goal to reduce the level of Winston's stress being achieved, while one or more of the longer-terms goals are not met.

A Set of Options

The third element of the decision frame is a set of options that are developed out of a picture of the situation and the decision makers' goals, circumscribed by the decision making context discussed in Chapter 1. Options are not objective facts waiting to be discovered but rather constructed by the decision makers within the limitations of their creativity and the contextual parameters in which they operate. The explicit identification and careful consideration of options is one of the most important aspects of sound decision making.

Identifying a set of options

By definition, there will always be at least two options in the decision situation, since only one option means there is no longer a decision to make. One of the first steps in a systematic approach to decision making is to conceive of the decision situation as consisting of a set of options, including doing nothing, something which at first sight may seem so obvious that it hardly warrants mentioning. In practice there can be a tendency to take a more pragmatic approach and have only one option in the frame at any one time, with no simultaneous appraisal of a range of options and the search for a solution ending as soon as a minimally satisfactory option is found. Within the decision making literature, this is referred to as 'satisficing' (see Beach, 1990, p. 106) and if the decision makers in the illustrative example were to adopt this pragmatic approach they may consider day care for Alice as a way of easing the situation. If this appeared to offer a satisfactory solution, the course of action would be taken; if not, it would be discarded without comparing it with other options. The order in which the alternatives are examined may be more or less haphazard, which can mean other more appropriate options may not be considered because an apparently satisfactory solution has already been found and the search finished. This is a method of decision making commonly adopted in everyday life: for example, buying the first satisfactory car found despite there being other car dealers to visit.

Basic options and sub-options

In decision analysis there is a limit to the number of options that can be usefully considered and it may be best to think in terms of broad courses of action, which will be referred to as basic options. It will usually be important to include the status quo as one of the options as this provides an important point of comparison. In Alice and Winston's situation, the basic options were identified as (i) to continue the current care plan unchanged; (ii) an intensification of the care plan while both Alice and Winston remain at home; or (iii) the introduction of residential care. A distinction can be made between the basic courses of action being considered and the various ways of improving the chances of them being successful by the provision or variation of services. To cope with the many possibilities, basic options can be considered to have sub-options. For example, there are many ways the care plan could be intensified, with the possibility that day care could be used in a number of different and imaginative ways. Whether all options are framed as basic options or whether the basic options are further broken down into sub-options is a matter of preference and the specific features of the decision situation. A manageable approach is to make the choice between the basic options and once that choice has been made to then decide between the sub-options.

What to include as options

What is included and what is excluded as options is an important consideration in the construction of the decision frame, one issue being whether to include patently undesirable options. Some options may be excluded from the systematic appraisal, on the basis that they are not compatible with the decision makers' values, goals or plans. In his *Image Theory* of decision making, Lee Roy Beach refers to this as the *compatibility test* (Beach, 1990, p. 71). Options are first matched to the decision makers' values, goals and plans, and only if they pass this compatibility test will they go on to be systematically appraised. A distinctive part of his theory is that if only one option survives the test, the next stage of decision making becomes unnecessary. If such a compatibility test were to be applied, residential care may have been dropped as an option. Although there is no point in including options that would not be followed under any circumstances, it can be a mistake within social work to be too quick to exclude options regarded as unattractive by one or more of the stakeholders. Much can be learnt from leaving undesirable options within the frame for systematic appraisal, as they can clarify the decision makers' thinking and be used as a comparison for other options. Unfortunately decision makers in social work often have no choice but to consider undesirable options, there being no favourable options open to them. Options that are not available may also be excluded from the frame, as when Preston made clear that him getting more involved was not an option.

Constraints and opportunities

Constraints and opportunities will operate in the construction of a set of options, that will require decision makers to be both creative and proactive. What is conceivable and what is considered feasible will be important influences on what is included. For example, the available resources are both a constraint and an opportunity for creativity. Feasibility and creativity form a two-way tension, with what is considered feasible being constrained by the limits of the decision makers' creativity and their creativity being constrained by the opportunities that exist. Acting as the purchaser of services, Bill is required to stay in budget and to be fair to other clients in the way that the finite resources are distributed. He believes day care can only become an option if Alice is considered to have an appropriate level of need, while Winston is unlikely to meet the agency's eligibility criteria. The quantity and quality of services available for purchasing is also an issue, as when the availability of a residential home that takes both people with and without dementia determines whether this could be an option within the decision frame. Bill needs to think about the use of the available resources in a creative way – for example, day care could be used a number of ways, each having a different impact on the decision situation. Either Alice could attend, Winston could attend or both of them could attend together.

In this particular situation Bill is in a good position in terms of resources available but this is by no means typical. One issue in social work is whether social workers passively accept the currently available resources as given or proactively endeavour to increase the level, range and quality of services available. This is not only an issue of political campaigning, but one of day-to-day practice. There are limits on what individual social workers, social work teams and agencies can do but they can either have a passive or proactive approach to the options. The role of the social service departments as 'enabling authorities' (Department of Health, 1989b, p. 17) gives a clear mandate to be proactive in the development of appropriate services, with private, voluntary, community groups and families needing support and encouragement in order to develop and sustain quality services.

Legislation and its associated procedures and guidance can also have an important role in the shaping of options. Options can take the form of following different legal or procedural routes, as for example in child care when the options may be whether to seek an Emergency Protection Order or not. Whether legal requirements are met is often an important consideration as to whether a course of action can be an option or not. Like resources, legislation is both a constraint and an opportunity for creativity. There can be a tendency to regard the law as a restricting force but it can also be considered as a vehicle for opening-up possibilities rather than closing them down (see Dalrymple and Burke, 1995). There is also the issue of how far social workers should just accept the legislative status quo or campaign for new laws or changes to the existing laws, when these do not work in practice or are a source of injustice. For example, the debate about whether protective legislation, similar to that which exists in respect of child protection, would help or hinder older people who are abused, particularly if it was not accompanied by increased resources (Biggs, Phillipson and Kingston, 1995, p. 113).

The options will not be appraised here, as that is the subject-matter of the next chapter, but it is important to note that considerable uncertainty surrounds them and that there will be differences in the value placed upon their possible outcomes. To take just one example, it is not known whether Alice attending day care would improve or exacerbate the situation further. Being transported to and from day care can be a further source of disorientation for people with dementia. If attendance at day care did cause Alice to become further disoriented, it may make the home situation worse with Winston needing to cope with even more difficult behaviour from his wife. Another factor to take into account is that what is considered a good outcome by one stake-holder may be considered a bad outcome by another. In this example, Winston may not consider Alice being away from him during the day in the same positive light as the other stakeholders.

Distortions in the Decision Frame

The decision makers' values, understandings and emotions contribute to the construction of the decision frame. In the case of the social worker, the professional nature of these values, understandings and emotions can be emphasised but the processes involved potentially operate to misrepresent people as well as accurately reflecting their uniqueness. This is true in two ways. Firstly, individual social workers have been brought up within and have internalised a particular culture and have human emotions, life concerns and personal idiosyncrasies. This means particular emphasis is needed in social work education on raising students' self-awareness of their own cultural backgrounds and social positions (Singh, 1996). Secondly, what passes for professional knowledge is not immune from beliefs prevalent in the dominant culture. Sociocultural beliefs concerning difference are a particular source of distortion, and critical self-awareness and reflective practice are needed to monitor whether decision frames are being built on an appropriate basis or not. There is potential for distortion in all decision situations, with one strong source being social differences between social workers and clients. The social differences between Bill and the other stakeholders mean there is a danger of distortion in the decision frame, and this section will examine the implications of Winston, Alice and Preston and the home help being black, while Bill is white. The issues of ethnicity, way of life and the recognition of racism will have important implications for the decision frame both in terms of a picture of the situation, decision goals and a set of options.

Impact of sociocultural beliefs on decision framing

The basis of a social worker's decision frame is ostensibly the application of professional values, knowledge and skills to what is known about a particular situation, with sociocultural beliefs being left out of the picture. Unfortunately these beliefs are so pervasive that they can play a significant role in the shaping of a decision frame and so the basis of a decision. The term sociocultural beliefs is used as a shorthand for those beliefs that are transmitted from generation to generation and internalised through early socialisation within a particular cultural context. In this sense, sociocultural beliefs are the taken-for-granted beliefs that often remained unquestioned and in the background of awareness. Due to their nature, sociocultural beliefs tend to be persistent and resistant to change, but they can be brought to awareness and modified or discarded. Nevertheless informal early learning during the formative years tends to be deeply embedded and individuals need to engage in a continuous struggle to unlearn, for example, racism. An important part of social work education is bringing sociocultural beliefs into awareness and unlearning those beliefs that negatively impact upon decision framing and the adoption of alternative beliefs in the form of professional values and knowledge (see Harlow and Hearn, 1996; Singh, 1996).

Of particular interest to decision framing in social work are sociocultural beliefs concerned with difference. Social workers practise in a multicultural and socially diverse society, yet they will have been brought up within a particular cultural context and have particular social characteristics. There are a number of potential sources of difference including: ethnicity, gender, 'race', age, sexuality, religion, class and other social dimensions. These differences are socially constructed and can be an important source of social identity. Their dominant social construction tends to be in terms of superiority and inferiority, but reconstruction on a more equal basis is possible. Bill, like every social worker, has a particular sociocultural profile made up of a number of sociocultural dimensions. The beliefs associated with this position can interfere with decision framing in a discriminatory and oppressive way. One area of skill within social work is the ability to work across difference (Narayan, 1989) without the negative impact of ethnocentrism, sexism, racism, homophobia, ageism and sectarianism.

Sociocultural differences and power

The issues of beliefs and attitudes towards difference go beyond the need for respect and sensitivity, as some decision makers have the power to impose their view within decision frames. The staffing of agencies can more or less reflect the distribution of power in the society. This means that there is a tendency for: adults to make decisions about children (Barford and Wattam, 1991), younger people to make decisions about older people (Biggs, 1992), white people to make decisions about black people (Dominelli, 1997b, p. 95), members of the ethnic majority to make decisions about members of ethnic minorities (Devore and Schlesinger, 1991) and straight people to make decisions in relation to gay people (Brown, 1998). Gender is more complex with both social workers and clients being predominantly women, but this is counterbalanced by social work management being dominated by men (Grimwood and Popplestone, 1993; Eley, 1989, p. 182). Social workers need to be continually aware of the danger of letting their own sociocultural beliefs negatively impact on decision framing and act on this awareness to counteract discriminatory and oppressive practices. To illustrate how sociocultural beliefs about difference can influence the basis of a decision frame the specific issue of racism will be examined, along with the associated but distinct issues of ethnocentrism, recognition of ethnicity, cultural superiority, being oversensitive of cultural difference and stereotyping. There is considerable potential for misunderstanding and confusion and a need to be clear about the different ways these can distort decision frames and how this can be counteracted.

Racism

Racism is a lens that distorts the features of the decision situation by interpreting them in terms of racial superiority and racial stereotypes. To be able to examine the ways racism can distort decision frames it is necessary to be clear what is being meant by the term. It is used here in a narrower sense than is often the case, with it being defined as a set of beliefs that attributes usually negatively evaluated characteristics to a group of people identified on the basis of some visible or imagined physical feature (adapted from Miles, 1989, p. 84). For example, within anti-black racism the physical feature, black colour of skin, is associated with negative characteristics, such as aggressiveness or lack of intelligence. Racism and the racialisation of social issues involves believing that there are different races of human beings with significant differences between them with some being superior to others. An anti-racist position is that there is only one race – that is, the human race – with no deep significant group differences being transmitted through genes and the notion of different biological races only existing within the various forms of racism. There are superficial biological differences between groups of people of different ethnic origin – such as colour of skin, colour of hair, and shape of eyes – that may signal differences in terms of identity and culture but these are not transmitted through human biology. As well as racism being a belief in the natural superiority or inferiority of certain 'racial' groups, it can take the form of xenophobia, based on a belief that it is *natural* to want to protect one's own social group from outsiders (Barker, 1981, p. 4).

Anti-black racism

Racism is a negative part of Bill's cultural inheritance that he needs
to be aware of and struggle against. The discussion here will be
confined to anti-black racism which is a legacy of European
colonialism and slavery, but other forms of racism exist and have
existed throughout history. It is through anti-black racism that
colour of skin gained significance with white European people
having the power to regard themselves as superior to black people,
which was eventually counteracted by black peoples' development
of a positive political identity built around their blackness (Ahmad,
1990, p. 2; Brah, 1992). Overt racism may not be prevalent within
social work, but often white decision makers are unaware, with
racism operating unintentionally (Dominelli, 1988) within decision
framing processes leading to discrimination and oppression in a
picture of the situation, decision goals and a set of options. Within
the process of developing an understanding and self-awareness of
racism, white social workers like Bill can become confused when
asked, on the one hand, to treat all people equally, with colour of
skin being an irrelevant factor and on the other hand to take into
account black people's experience of racism and black perspectives.
What is needed is a deeper understanding of the nature of racism
and its impact and the importance of ethnicity. With such an
understanding it becomes clear that these two requests are not
contradictory, with anti-racists asking white social workers to:

- confront their own racism that they will have learnt by virtue of
  being brought up within a culture imbued with racism;
- work within their agencies to counteract any racism that has been
  institutionalised within policies, procedures and established ways
  of doing things;
- monitor their own practice and practice knowledge in relation to
  the potential for racism to either creep in or be endemic;
- recognise and be sensitive to black people having a different
  ethnicity to white people and to other black people of a different
  ethnicity;
- recognise and counteract the dominance of white culture and
  white ways of looking at things and value other perspectives
  including black perspectives;
- be sensitive to and take into account the fact that black people
  can experience racism on a day-to-day basis and be proactive in

endeavouring to counteract this oppression. This includes recognising that racism can be the cause of the difficulties that bring people into contact with social workers in the first place. Being on the receiving end of racism on a daily basis can be a cause of stress that in turn exacerbates other problems people may have. For example, Winston's difficult task of caring for Alice may be made more difficult by the racial harassment of local white youth.

Related to and interacting with and within racism are ethnocentrism, non-recognition of the importance of ethnicity, cultural superiority and stereotyping. A clear distinction is needed between these different discriminatory processes if decision frames are not to be distorted.

Ethnocentrism

The terms culture and ethnicity are highly problematic and are used in a number of ways. In this discussion the term culture is used to denote a distinct way of life (Williams, 1981, p. 11) and ethnicity as a sense of shared descent (Smith, 1986, p. 192). There is a considerable overlap between the terms, but in this complex area it is helpful to examine them as separate issues. In a multicultural society there are a number of different ways of life and it is not uncommon for social workers to be culturally different from the clients they come in contact with. The views social workers and clients have of the world have been shaped by the culture in which they were brought up. There is a danger that decision framers take an ethnocentric view and regard their own way of life as the natural way of doing things, which leads to the making of assumptions and insensitivity. Decision makers have a right to their own way of life but in a multicultural society there needs to be awareness and appreciation that different people have different ways of living and different ways of doing things. Once an awareness, understanding and valuing of the existence of different ways of life has been achieved there is a danger of only conceptualising other cultures in terms of defects and ignoring their strengths (Ahmed, 1986, p. 141). There is also the danger of an overreliance on cultural explanations of problems and ignoring emotional, interpersonal and structural factors (Ahmed, 1986, p. 140). Culture sets an important context for understanding decision situations but it is only one of a number of important factors to be taken into consideration.

Recognition of ethnicity

Within a decision frame there needs to be a recognition of the importance of ethnicity for people's sense of identity and belonging. Ethnicity can be defined as a sense of shared descent and common cultural heritage (Smith, 1986, p. 192) and is often a complex mix of identification with descent from a particular way of life, continent, nation state, country, region, religion or some combination of these. Within a world of both voluntary and forced movements of people, ethnicity can be based on identification with membership of a diaspora, for example, the African-Caribbean diaspora (Hall, 1992). Both social workers and clients have ethnicity, but some people have more explicit recognition of the contribution their ethnicity has to their overall conception of themselves. Ethnicity is often thought of as African descent, African-Caribbean descent, White European descent or South Asian descent, but a sense of ethnicity can be quite specific to a particular region or nation state and people who appear similar on the surface may be ethnically very different. Alice and Winston very much identify with the island of St Lucia which they had hoped to return to one day; consequently, Winston resented Bill referring to him as Jamaican. A person's ethnicity is important because it is part of their sense of identity and members of different ethnic groups can have different beliefs and practices in relation to life events such as death, dying and bereavement.

Cultural superiority and being oversensitive to cultural difference

From particular cultural positions some differences between ways of life are highly controversial, being seen as going against some core value that transcends culture. For example, regarding the role of women in a particular culture as oppressed, or a standard of cleanliness as being too high or too low, or a pattern of family life as being irresponsible. There are at least two positions in relation to clashes of cultural values. The first is *cultural relativity*, with all cross-cultural evaluations being seen as questionable. Within this position, actions or lack of actions that may be labelled abuse or neglect by outsiders should only be judged within that culture's own standards. This might involve, for example, accepting a higher level of physical chastisement from an African-Caribbean father than a white European father because such punishment is thought to be (erroneously or not) part of a particular culture's way of doing things.

The other position is of *value absolutism* with core values being absolute rather than relative, with some cultural practices being regarded as oppressive and wrong – for example, female circumcision being child abuse. As it is impossible to completely transcend culture, such judgements are associated with moral superiority of one kind or another. Within social work both relativism and absolutism are hazardous. There is a need for a balance between sensitivity to different ways of doing things and a clear sense of what is unacceptable (Stevenson, 1989, p. 201). To some extent what is acceptable and what is unacceptable is defined by the laws of the nation state in which the social worker is practising, although the fairness of laws can be questioned both from inside and outside nation states. Nevertheless laws need interpretation and as we have seen, of necessity, there need to be large areas of discretion in social work; so the potential exists for the twin hazards of cultural superiority and accepting the unacceptable as cultural practice. For example, white social workers rescuing young Asian women from arranged marriages (Ahmed, 1986, p. 145) or failing to protect black children from abuse for fear of being labelled racist (Modi, Marks and Wattley, 1995, p. 99; Adams, 1996a, p. 88).

Stereotyping and stereotypes

Another source of distortion within decision frames is the use of cultural stereotypes, for example, using stereotypical images of the African-Caribbean family or the Asian family (Ahmad, 1990, p. 9). Bill may have had a stereotype of African-Caribbean people as having less need of services given their greater commitment to care for older people compared with white European people (Atkin and Rollings, 1996, p. 76). There is no agreement as to the precise use of the terms stereotyping and stereotype (Leyens, Yzerbyt and Schadron, 1994, p. 11), but for the purpose of our discussion *stereotyping* will be used to denote a process of thinking about and feeling towards a person and their situation on the basis of their supposed membership of a category – for example, African-Caribbean man. A *stereotype* is the content of this category, the characteristics that members of the category are presumed to have in common: for example, Asian families look after their own (Patel, 1990, p. 30); old people are cantankerous or senile; black men are lazy and aggressive; the African-Caribbean family is disorganised. If stereotypes are operating there may be more readiness to see Winston as a violent man because he is a black male. The use of stereotypes involves placing people in categories, but there is a difficulty and tension concerning the use of categories within social work. As we have seen, a decision frame is a simplification of a complex reality and will of necessity make use of categories – for example, child in need or adult at risk. Social workers may aim to frame decisions, as much as is possible, on the basis of the uniqueness of the people and their situations, but it is impossible to capture this in all its complexity and intricacy. It may be a practical impossibility to develop a decision frame without using categories, but how categories are constructed is an issue – for example, whether the characteristics of the category are regarded as fixed or as contingent on the circumstances (Brah, 1992).

As well as the issue of how the categories are constructed, there is an important distinction between the use of categories to integrate a range of information or to extrapolate from one piece of information (Leyens, Yzerbyt and Schadron, 1994, p. 204). Using categories to integrate a vast range of information is central to decision framing, for example, referring to Alice as being in the middle stages of dementia. This needs to be contrasted with stereotyping – the use of a category to infer presumed characteristics from one piece of information. This involves inferring from knowledge of a person's age, the colour of their skin, ethnicity or their nationality, certain presumed characteristics – for example, Winston is a black man so he is aggressive. Stereotypes are crude, arbitrary and inaccurate and have no validity, with the categories being too broad for the people placed within them to have attributes in common. Such stereotypes usually have negative characteristics but can contain positive characteristics, for example, because Alice is of African-Caribbean descent she may have been seen as the matriarchal head of the family. Part of the operation of sets of beliefs like racism, sexism, ageism and homophobia is the use of crude stereotypes.

Beliefs imported from the social worker's personal life

Sociocultural beliefs are not the only source of distortion in decision frames, as beliefs can be imported from social workers' personal lives. These can make a positive contribution to a decision frame, but there is the potential for them to be a source of distortion. Social workers learn about life issues and processes during their training and through reflective practice but beliefs about life are also formed through specific personal experiences. Ideas about birth and death, bringing up children, relationships and growing old are developed through life experience, and social workers may believe that if a solution worked for them it will work for others. Social workers may be tempted to think if they had a certain experience of a life event in their personal life, for example, divorce, other people's experience will be the same. Self-awareness of personal beliefs and the way they potentially distort decision framing is important, as there is a danger that social workers are unaware of the impact they can have on their professional work.

This is not to say that social workers cannot use their personal experience of life in their work. If they have satisfactorily resolved particular life issues, potentially this could put them in a stronger position to empower people experiencing similar difficulties. Former drug abusers may be in a better position to empower those who want to stop abusing drugs, as the insight and understanding gained from life experiences can make a positive contribution. Clients want their predicament understood and the ability to empathise is regarded as important as when parents involved in child protection situations ask the social worker if he or she has children of their own. Nevertheless, people's experience of life events is variable and unique and although having direct experience of life events can contribute to sound decision framing it needs to be done without the expectation that others will have the same experience. This may only be possible if the issue has been worked through in a way that promotes insight and understanding.

Particular life experiences can also have a negative influence on decision framing when social workers import feelings and attitudes associated with unresolved life issues into the decision frame. For example, Bill's father is in residential care having struggled at home after experiencing a stroke and the death of his wife. As a defence against feelings of guilt, Bill may overemphasise the positive benefits of residential care and the dangers of staying in one's own home. He may overidentify with Preston who wants his mother to go into a home and so lose a sense of balance and impartiality.

The impact life experience has on a person's attitudes can vary as when they advocate or react against the way they were brought up. For example, Bill had a difficult relationship with his own father, which may distort his attitude towards Winston. The important thing is that Bill is aware of his beliefs and emotions and through self-awareness can counteract any negative impact they might have on the decision frame.

CHAPTER SUMMARY AND KEY POINTS

This chapter has focused on framing the decision situation, with the decision frame being identified as consisting of three parts: a picture of the decision situation, decision goals, and a set of options. Through the decision makers' values, understandings and emotions, a frame of the decision situation is built up but inappropriate beliefs can potentially cause distortions that result in discrimination and oppression.

When framing the decision situation social workers, together with clients and other stakeholders, need to:

- develop a holistic picture of the situation which takes into account all relevant factors;
- identify decision goals;
- clearly identify a set of options; and
- consider potential distortions to the decision frame.

Issues and tensions when framing the decision situation include:

- whether the decision frame is best considered an 'objective picture' or 'artistic creation';
- what to do when there are differences between the social workers' understandings of decision situations and those of clients; and
- how decision frames can be constructed without the distorting effects of racism and other forms of oppressive beliefs.

7

Choice of Options

Central to sound decision making is being aware of and explicit about how choices are being made. There are two sets of ethics that influence making a choice in social work, those concerned with achieving a good outcome and those concerned with doing what is right, while emotions can push decision makers in various and at times contradictory directions. What is needed is a systematic appraisal of the options on some appropriate basis, but there is considerable potential for confused, inconsistent and vague thinking. In this chapter potential bases of choice will be divided into three categories: what the possible outcomes of the options are thought to be including the question of risk; whether the options are considered 'right' or 'wrong' in themselves; and the emotional appeal or repulsion of the options. For the sake of clarity, the reasons for the choice of an option will be treated as separate categories, but they are not mutually exclusive and in practice all three can be involved in the appraisal of the options.

ILLUSTRATIVE EXAMPLE

Zena has just turned 16 years old, and is a British Asian woman, whose bilingual parents emigrated from Pakistan some time ago. She was accommodated by the local authority when she ran away from home, and became involved in prostitution after her parents tried to stop her seeing her white boyfriend. Her father refused to have her back home because of the shame he felt Zena had brought to the family, but is now beginning to soften his attitude. Margaret, the social worker working with Zena and her family, is of white European origin. Zena has been placed with South Asian foster parents, while work towards her reconciliation with her family is undertaken. Unfortunately the placement is not going well at present, there being tension between Zena and the foster father. The foster mother is wondering whether she will be able to cope with the situation much longer and a meeting has been arranged of all those concerned to discuss whether the placement can continue or if Zena should return home. Margaret is endeavouring to work in partnership with Zena, her parents and the foster parents, but her foremost consideration is Zena's welfare. Zena has declined the services of an independent advocate, feeling she is well able to put her own views forward.

At the meeting, the stakeholders were able to agree on goals and options as follows:

shorter-term goal: for the placement not to break down.
longer-term goal: that Zena is able to develop, in a safe and stable environment, into an emotionally and socially well adjusted adult with a clear sense of identity.

Options

• to stay in the present foster home;
• to return home.

Both options were considered in the context of what plans could be made to maximise the likelihood of their success. For example, the option of the placement continuing was in the context of a series of family meetings being held to focus on the points of tension within the foster family. Each option involved varying degrees of uncertainty about whether it would provide stability and a suitable environment in which Zena could develop.

Potential Distortions to the Frame

As the decision situation occurs in a white-dominated society, racism (particularly of the more subtle variety) may have a negative impact on Margaret's thinking and the nature of the resources available (Dominelli, 1997, p. 32). There is also danger of her taking an ethnocentric view about human development, family life and growing up. Stereotypes may come into the picture – for example, a stereotype of the 'Asian Family' as being self-sufficient (Atkin and Rollings, 1996, p. 76). There is also the danger of overreliance on cultural explanations of the difficulties faced by Zena and her family (Ahmed, 1986, p. 148). The age difference between Zena and the other participants could be a source of distortion if the 'adults' use their power to either prevent Zena from putting forward her point of view or not taking it seriously (Barford and Wattam, 1991).

The Possible Outcomes of the Options

The first basis for choosing an option to be discussed is that the chosen course of action is likely to have a good outcome. This is a strand of the utilitarian school of moral philosophy, where no particular course of action is seen as 'right' or 'wrong' in itself, but only as 'good' by virtue of its outcome. This should *not* be confused with the strand of utilitarian thought concerned with the promotion of the common good, the focus being the specific consequences of an option on the lives of the people involved (Rhodes, 1985, p. 102). The notion of good outcome may at times be misleading, because it is not uncommon in social work for all the options to be considered as having potentially negative outcomes. The question in these circumstances becomes which is the least detrimental outcome rather than which is the most beneficial (Goldstein, Freud and Solnit, 1973). Nevertheless one of a social worker's professional duties is to work towards good outcomes and in child care it is a legal duty to work towards good outcomes for the children concerned. Choosing an option that will have a good outcome involves issues of value and uncertainty, which will be explored by examining three methods of helping decision makers make a choice: a balance sheet, a decision tree and risk assessment. Choosing an option in these ways is an example of the use of analysis to make a decision and, as discussed in Chapter 5, this will take time and may not always be helpful. Rather than breaking down the decision situation into different components, intuition or a heuristic short cut can be used (see Chapter 5).

Balancing the consequences

Rarely will an outcome of a decision be wholly good or wholly bad; rather it will have a mixture of consequences, both good and bad, which means that judging which option is likely to have a good outcome involves balancing the positive anticipations against the negative anticipations. As well as positive and negative, a number of other terms are used for analysing consequences each of which reflects a different emphasis, such as pros and cons, benefits and costs, gains and losses, desired and undesired, useful and not useful or pluses and minuses. One way of analysing the possible consequences of a set of options is to construct a balance-sheet of dangers and potential benefits. The terms dangers and potential benefits

FIGURE 7.1   *A simple balance sheet*

option	potential benefits	dangers
stay in foster home	to be relatively safe to have relative stability	unplanned move triggered by crisis Zena not living with her family having a long-term impact on her development
return home	family and community provide a supportive base Zena able to develop her ethnic identity	that Zena will run away again that she will become reinvolved in prostitution family relationships will deteriorate to a point that they become irreconcilable

have the advantage of highlighting that the consequences are possibilities rather than certainties, something a simple balance-sheet approach, as shown in Figure 7.1, may otherwise not take account of. Balancing positives against negatives becomes more complex when there is more than one stakeholder involved, as different people may place a different value on the same consequence. The consequences of Zena's successful return home may be her reconciliation with her family and her growing autonomy being checked, which Zena's family regard as positive consequences, whereas Zena regards them as negative. Even when decisions are taken by single stakeholders alone, for example the client, they can have considerable ambivalence about a consequence, making it difficult for them to place a value on it.

When faced with a difficult choice there are some advantages to constructing a balance sheet, as they clearly set out the positives and negatives of particular courses of action. Considering the different aspects of the options means that decision makers become explicitly aware of why, on balance, they choose a particular option and so are less likely to regret a decision. Nevertheless, it would be misleading to simply add up the number of negatives and take them away from the number of positives in a mechanistic way, since the different consequences are unlikely to be of equal value with some consequences having more weight than others. On the basis of the way the stakeholders in the example have set out their balance sheet, the *stay in the foster home* option would be chosen, it being associated with two potential benefits and two dangers, whereas the *return home* option, while also having two potential benefits, has three dangers. As the number of positives and negatives can be arbitrary, being the result of the decision makers' thought processes and interactions, a simple numerical approach is inappropriate and a more qualitative consideration is needed.

Evaluative dimensions

One way of overcoming the danger of the number of positives, relative to the number of negatives, being used in a mechanistic way to make a choice, is to analyse each option on a given number of dimensions. Evaluative dimensions are indicators used to gauge the value of possible outcomes. They are what are considered to have importance in the situation and are usually a more specific formulation of the decision makers' goals. Their identification involves issues of value and they may be an area of contention between the stakeholders. In the example, the evaluative dimensions were identified as Zena's safety, the stability of her living situation, Zena developing a clear sense of identity, her social and emotional adjustment and her family relationships. These dimensions can be used to analyse the possible consequences of the various options and eventually will be used to evaluate the actual outcome sometime in the future (see Chapter 8). The balance sheet can now be set out in a way that is less likely to lead to a mechanistic numerical approach and more likely to encourage a consideration of the relative qualitative aspects of the consequences and the uncertainty as to how they will actually unfold (see Figure 7.2). It needs to be remembered that the potential benefits and dangers featured in Figure 7.2 are not, nor can they be, established facts. Rather, they represent the beliefs and values of the decision makers. For further discussion of the general use of decisional balance sheets to make decisions, see Janis and Mann (1977, chapter 6).

FIGURE 7.2 *A balance sheet using evaluative dimensions*

option	potential benefits	dangers
stay in foster home (evaluative dimensions)		
personal safety	to be relatively safe	there may be some unknown risk within the foster home
stability of living situation	have relative stability	unplanned move triggered by crisis
sense of identity	to live with a family who share her ethnicity	Zena's rebellion against her cultural roots compounded
social and emotional adjustment	to live in a family environment	Zena not living with her family having a long term impact on her development
family relationships	to mend family relationships while not living at home	Zena and family drifting apart
return home (evaluative dimensions)		
personal safety	Zena has the protection of her family and community	that she will become reinvolved in prostitution
stability of living situation	long term stability	that Zena will run away again
sense of identity	Zena able to develop her ethnic identity	Zena rejects her community further
social and emotional adjustment	family and community provide a supportive base from which to develop	Zena has her social and emotional development checked
family relationships	family relationships improve on her rejoining the household	family relationships will deteriorate to a point that they become irreconcilable

Analysing uncertainty

Although the strength of a balance sheet is its relative straightfor-
wardness and the way it highlights how outcomes can be associated
with a mixture of consequences, it does not fully take into account
the uncertainty about what will actually happen when a particular
course of action is taken. The outcomes of courses of action are
always uncertain, it not being possible to predict with certainty
whether an option will lead to a good or detrimental outcome. For
example, it is uncertain whether Zena's return home would be
successful or not, as it is not known whether she will settle down
or run away again. In the analysis of uncertainty it is important to
be clear about the distinction between a *decision outcome* which
occurs after an option has been implemented and will be discussed
in the next chapter and the *possible outcomes* which are the range of
outcomes that may occur when a particular course of action is
followed. An analysis of uncertainty involves identifying the possible outcomes of a set of options and deciding which option gives the
best chance of a good outcome occurring by taking the following
steps.

For *each* option:

- identify the *possible outcomes*;
- place a *value* on each possible outcome;
- estimate the *likelihood* of each possible outcome occurring; and
- choose an option that gives the best chance of a good outcome.

Identifying the possibilities

Social workers, clients and other stakeholders are unable to predict
the future, so there is always a degree of uncertainty as to what the
outcome of an option will be. This uncertainty needs to be made
explicit within the analysis of options. For example, it cannot be
known with certainty how things will turn out if Zena stays in her
foster home. Judging the possibilities of what may happen needs
care and thought, but there is a danger that the uncertainty involved
will not be made explicit. People can experience considerable
discomfort when asked what the possibilities are, as explicitly
identifying implicit predictions brings home to those involved the
uncertainty in which they operate. There can also be a contrary

tendency of being too ready to predict outcomes when people operate within a spurious certainty – either through professional arrogance or misplaced confidence in risk assessment (see Stanley and Manthorpe, 1997, p. 31).

Uncertainty can most clearly be represented by means of a decision tree, like the one given in Figure 7.3, which can be thought of as three columns – the options, the possibilities and the outcome. Decision makers need to simplify complex decision situations, and when there is uncertainty about the outcome of an option, they need to concentrate on a limited number of possibilities. The least complex way of doing this is for the uncertainty to be associated with two possibilities: the course of action being successful or the course of action being unsuccessful, leading to either a good outcome or a bad outcome. In our example, if Zena stays in her foster home, it could at least partially meet her needs or break down. The number of possibilities of an option is a matter of decision framing and may need to be more than two. For example, a third possible outcome could be added, the foster home not breaking down but failing to meet Zena's needs, which would be represented in the decision diagram by a third branch on the *stay in the present foster home* option. Representing possible outcomes in the form of a decision tree gives the opportunity to decision makers to clarify the issues of uncertainty involved, but it also imposes a structure on the decision situation that may become set by virtue of the fact of being written down. Even simple decision trees take considerable effort to construct and any move beyond the simple can easily lead to a confusing array of branches and sub-branches.

Placing a value on possible outcomes

When referring to the value of both possible and actual outcomes, for the most part, the terms good and bad have been used. Although this is a rather crude dichotomy, it does have the advantage of enabling the discussion of value to proceed. It needs to be remembered that what is a good and a bad outcome are not discoverable facts but matters of judgement and value, about which stakeholders may disagree. A good outcome will be defined as when the consequences of decision implementation are considered beneficial and a bad outcome when the consequences are considered detrimental. The identification of what are regarded as good outcomes and bad outcomes is problematic, particularly when other stakeholders are involved with the client in deciding what to do. Who actually determines the value of an outcome is an issue of great importance, with adult clients usually being in a position to decide for themselves what a good outcome would be. For example, an adult client terminally ill in hospital may regard dying in his or her own home as a good outcome, despite death usually being regarded as a bad outcome.

The value child clients place on the possible outcomes needs to be taken into account but may not determine the choice of option. For example, in our case study Zena does not regard running away from home again and returning to prostitution as a bad outcome. Decision makers need to be clear that, other things being equal, clients have the right to define good outcomes for themselves. This means that in the case of adult clients and young people who are considered to have sufficient level of understanding to determine their own future, no assumptions can be made as to what they will regard as a good or a bad outcome. When the client is a younger child, it may be justified to think in terms of what is in their best interests but this is not an entirely straightforward matter (see Lansdown, 1995, p. 27). If the stakeholders are working together, the identification of good and bad outcomes becomes more problematic and may need to be the subject of negotiation. When the stakeholders have different values and beliefs, the possible outcomes will need to be considered from a number of points of view, including that of the clients, social workers and the other stakeholders.

The decision tree shown in Figure 7.3 has been constructed so that each option has a good outcome and a bad outcome. To be able to decide which option gives the best chance of a good outcome, it is necessary to go a step further and determine the relative value of the possible outcomes in relation to each other. This may be a relatively straightforward process when a single client is making a decision for themselves, but when there are a number of stakeholders involved it can involve complex negotiation in which consensus may never be reached. The stakeholders in the example need to know whether they value *Zena's successful return home* more highly than her *successfully staying in the foster home* and whether *the foster home suddenly breaking down* is a worse outcome than *her running away from home again*. The stakeholders can make a start by individually listing the possible outcomes in the order of

FIGURE 7.3   *A decision tree*

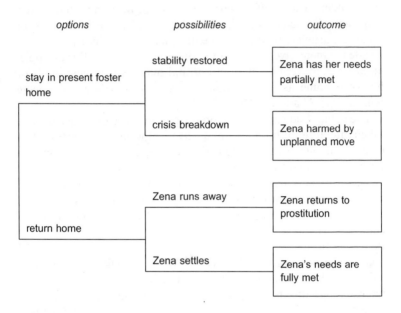

value they would place them. Zena's order was the placement being a success (first), running away from home (second), placement breaking down (third) and successful return home (last). Whereas the order of the other stakeholders was, successful return home (first), placement being a success (second), placement breaking down (third) and running away from home (last). It is possible to quantify these relative values by awarding them points out of ten, or by the adoption of more sophisticated methods (see Dowie, 1992c, p. 73), but it is beyond the scope of this book to examine the issues involved in doing this.

Estimating the likelihood of possible outcomes

Decision analysis would be relatively straightforward if it was solely a case of choosing the option that had the most valued outcome. Unfortunately uncertainty means that there are a number of possible outcomes of an option and it is not known for certain which one will occur. To take decision analysis further, the trouble-some concept of *likelihood* needs to be introduced. The terms likelihood, probability and chance will be taken as synonymous with the term likelihood favoured, as it is less associated with mathematics compared with probability and less associated with gambling compared with chance. The concept of likelihood needs to be introduced despite its difficulties because it enables decision makers to be explicit about their estimates of the chances of possible outcomes occurring. There is no need to be frightened of the term likelihood but every reason to take great care in its use.

The likelihood of an uncertain event occurring is the degree of possibility that event will happen. It is common in social work for this to be referred to in terms of being very high, high, low or very low. The basis of estimates of likelihood are controversial, as valid and reliable actuarial knowledge of how frequently an outcome is likely to occur in particular circumstances is rarely available. Such knowledge would need to be based on systematic and extensive research into what has happened in numerous past situations which, with a few exceptions (for example, Monahan and Steadman, 1994), is not available for the types of prediction needed in social work. Social workers estimating the likelihood of an event happening are likely to need to use their professional judgement, which may take the form of what Schon referred to as *reflection-in-action* and *knowledge-in-action* (Schon, 1995, pp. 49–69). These judgements need to be informed and defensible, being based on both knowledge of the situation, practice wisdom and any valid research evidence that is available. It is more accurate to refer to likelihood as being *estimated* rather than calculated, as it is a question of judgement and belief, rather than actuarial calculation (J. Adams, 1995, p. 26). Margaret estimates that Zena's return home at this stage is very unlikely to succeed and she needs to be able to explain why to the other stakeholders. With some thought she should be able to trace the reasons for her judgement and the other decision makers can judge whether they find these convincing or not.

The issue of quantification

Margaret is comfortable referring to Zena's return being very unlikely to succeed, but when asked by the team manager to be more precise about how unlikely, Margaret is reluctant to put a figure on it. As well as dangers, there are some advantages in quantifying estimates of likelihood, for although decision makers may appear to agree on a particular event being, for example, very unlikely, they may in fact attach a very different meaning to this term. For one person it may mean something like a one per cent chance, but for another a 25 per cent chance (Dowie, 1992a, p. 39). An argument against placing a numerical value on estimates of likelihood, is that there may be a tendency for decision makers to be seduced by the numbers and forget that they are dealing with matters of judgement and belief; they may come to spuriously regard them as somehow scientific or objective statements of fact.

Hogarth (1987, p. 245) states that 'the most difficult facet of probability assessment is asking yourself what you really think' and Margaret does find it difficult to be more precise about her belief that Zena's return home is unlikely to succeed. Her team manager tries to help her by confirming with her that she does not believe that it is a certainty that Zena's return home will be unsuccessful, but that it is more likely to fail than to succeed. When asked how much more likely, again she is reluctant to put a figure on it, but was prepared to say that it is nearer certainty than a 50/50 chance. In the end Margaret and the team manager agreed that her estimation of the likelihood of Zena returning to prostitution if she returned home at this point in time was in the order of an 80 per cent chance, giving her return home only a 20 per cent chance of success. It is a matter of controversy as to whether these estimations already exist implicitly in the minds of decision makers or whether they are a product of the analysis process itself. If it is the former, it could be argued that it is appropriate that they are made explicit and so be open to scrutiny. If it is the latter, the question becomes whether it is appropriate to encourage estimates of likelihood in this way, the answer revolving around the issue of their validity. They can make a positive contribution to the decision making process if they have a sound basis, but if they are unfounded guesses they may hinder sound decision making.

Choosing an option that gives the best chance of a good outcome

So far the analysis has helped the decision makers clarify what they regard as:

- the possible outcomes of each option;
- their relative value;
- their view of the relative likelihood of them occurring.

This is the minimum amount of clarity needed in order to be able to base the choice of options on the most likely to give a good outcome. These different aspects will need to be combined to give the most favourable option in terms of giving the best chance of a good outcome. Zena's successful return home was the most valued outcome, but it was estimated as the least likely to happen. By contrast, although regaining the stability of her present foster home was less valued, it was considered more likely to happen. As a consequence, the result of this analysis is likely to be the *staying in foster home* option being favoured over the *returning home* option. If the decision makers had quantified the value and likelihood of the possible outcomes they could have calculated what in the decision making literature is referred to as *the expected utility* of the option and chosen the option with the greatest expected utility. This compounds the issues involved in quantifying value and likelihood referred to above and space does not allow a detailed discussion, but for a clear procedural account in the context of medical decision making, see Dowie (1992b).

Assessment of Risk

So far the choice of options has been based on an attempt to identify the option that gives the best chance of a good outcome, but another way of looking at this is to decide on the basis of a risk assessment. Risk has the two components of possible outcome already considered – value and likelihood – with a tendency to only focus on exposure to chance of loss. Solely focusing on a fear of loss is a comparatively recent development (Parton, 1996, p. 105) and the association of risk with both the possibilities of loss and gain needs to be re-established. Risk assessment can either be full or partial, depending on whether all options within the decision frame are subjected to assessment and whether opportunities as well as risks are included in the analysis. A full assessment will have similarities to the analysis of uncertainty already discussed, whereas a partial risk assessment may only focus on one option and be preoccupied with potential losses to the neglect of potential gains. In deciding a course of action, decision makers can be concerned with being safe or achieving benefits or a balance between the two. If risks are necessary in bringing about good outcomes, decisions need to be taken on a careful assessment of the balance of risks and opportunities, rather than being unthinkingly reckless or over cautious. As Carson states, social workers need to be more forthright in arguing that the justification for taking risks is the benefits that are sought, with risk taking defined as 'choosing to act to achieve beneficial results in an awareness that harms might result' (Carson, 1988, p. 319).

Uses of risk assessment

A distinction needs to be made between risk assessment as a basis of making a choice between options and other uses to which it can be put. In a political and economic context in which welfare services are being targeted, risk assessment can be used to sort the *high-risk* cases from the rest (Parton, 1998, p. 18), while preventative and therapeutic work are given low priority. Risk assessment can also be used as the basis for risk management, a process of managing the exposure of a chance of loss which may involve the support, monitoring and surveillance of situations. Related to risk management is risk minimisation which Ann Davis describes as an approach which focuses on a small minority of potentially dangerous people and subjects them to surveillance and control. Denise Tanner states 'risk assessment and risk management are concepts concerned with identification and management of social problems rather than their treatment' (Tanner, 1998, p. 16), but risk assessment is not inevitably associated with risk management. It has a potential role in a risk taking approach in which risk is viewed as an inevitable part of life if people are to have autonomy, choice and social participation (Davis, 1996).

Strengths/hazards analysis

Making a judgement as to whether a course of action is justified on the basis of the potential benefits it offers, despite the risks it entails, can be aided by a strengths/hazards analysis. Such an analysis draws from the work of Brearley (1982), who used the term *danger* to denote the future feared undesirable event – that is, the possible bad outcome. For example, in the *staying in the foster home* option, the danger was identified as a sudden and irretrievable breakdown of the placement. The terms *hazards* and *strengths* are used to denote the features of the present situation which affect the likelihood of the danger occurring; hazards increase the likelihood of

FIGURE 7.4   *A stengths/hazards analysis*

'Staying in foster home' option	
Present	**Future**
hazards difficulties in relationship between foster parents Zena's history of running away	*danger* foster home will suddenly break down
strengths experienced foster family foster family from same ethnic background	*benefit* a caring and stable base to work towards Zena's reconciliation with her family

the danger happening, while strengths offer some protection against it happening. Their identification gives a potential basis for making a judgement as to the likelihood of whether an option will have a good or bad outcome and can encourage a proactive approach to risk rather than a passive one, with efforts made to reduce the hazards in the situation and increase the strengths although some factors by their nature will not be amenable to change.

Hazards and strengths can be put alongside the potential dangers and benefits to form a hazards/strengths analysis such as the one given in Figure 7.4. One of the weaknesses of Brearley's influential 1982 work on risk was that *benefits* were not given an equal place alongside *dangers* in the analysis of risk. All options under consideration would need to be analysed in terms of hazards and strengths and Figure 7.4 gives such an analysis in respect of the *staying in foster home* option. The potential benefit is included alongside the potential danger, with the identification of related strengths and hazards being a matter of judgement. Figure 7.4 identifies 'difficulties in the relationship between the foster parents' as a hazard while a strength is 'the foster family's successful experience of fostering difficult children'. What are designated as hazards and strengths and whether they provide a reliable and valid way of estimating the likelihood of a danger/benefit happening is problematic, requiring careful critical reflection and wide consultation.

Risk factors

A distinction can be made between the unique situational hazards considered above and more general risk factors thought to give rise to particular dangers. The latter, also referred to as risk indicators or risk markers, have been increasingly compiled into checklists, that are incorporated within risk assessment schedules, protocols and instruments to be used as tools to make predictions (see Kemshall, 1996; Monahan and Steadman, 1994). Although the prospect of being able to assess the likelihood of dangers occurring is seductive, these instruments are often considered to have limited reliability (Stanley and Manthorpe, 1997, p. 33). A risk-factor checklist is a list of factors thought to indicate the likelihood of a particular danger – such as child abuse, suicide, violence and other harmful behaviour – occurring or recurring. While specific situational hazards are identified through professional assessment and are based on professional judgement and practice wisdom, general risk factors in theory could be based on scientific knowledge of cause and effect, actuarial data about what has happened in numerous similar situations in the past, or the best available professional knowledge.

One of the problems with risk factors, as opposed to situational specific hazards, is they can be given a spurious and unwarranted scientific or actuarial status. There is no scientific knowledge of cause-and-effect relationships between risk factors and dangers. Recursive loops are more characteristic of the social world, than the lineal unidirectional relationships of cause and effect. What research has been done into risk factors tends to be retrospective and so affected by a number of serious methodological difficulties. Prospective research is regarded as a more valid way to identity factors associated with particular dangers but is less common and has its own inherent difficulties (Dingwall, 1989, p. 38). Often what are regarded as risk factors have their source in expert judgement or spurious inferences from retrospective data. When risk assessment schedules consist of the best professional knowledge available, including the findings of valid research, they can be useful aids to professional decision making – for example, Michael Sheppard's schedule for assessing compulsory mental health admissions (Sheppard, 1990). The danger is they are used in a mechanistic or technical way, giving rise to a spurious misplaced confidence (Wald

FIGURE 7.5 *The reliability of risk assessment*

		Risk Assessment Result Prediction of likelihood of danger occuring	
		positive (high risk)	negative (low risk)
Outcome	danger occurs/ would have occured	true positive	false negative
	danger does *not* occur/would *not* have occurred	false positive	true negative

and Woolverton, 1990) and in the process undermine professional judgement and the development of professional expertise.

The issue is not so much whether checklists are used or not, but rather what their appropriate role is within professional social work. There is a difference between using checklists in a mechanical way to make a decision and their use in aiding the formation of professional judgement. Risk factors have a role in focusing judgement on what is currently the best available professional knowledge as to what factors are associated with particular dangers. They are misused when the number of factors present are added up to form an accumulative risk score without evidence that they are valid indicators that are independent of each other. In the context of the USA, where risk assessment instruments are extensively used by agencies, Wald and Woolverton (1990) argue that workers should not be bound to make decisions based on an individual's risk score or limited to considering only those factors on the list. They go on to state that risk checklists can enable

> workers to apply more consistently whatever clinical criteria they use in making individual decisions, and/or to get all workers within an agency to focus on those factors that are believed, on the basis of research or expert judgement, to be most relevant in the decisions that are being made. (Wald and Woolverton, 1990, p. 489)

Reliability of risk assessment

The issue of reliability of risk assessment is relevant whether professional judgement or checklists are used alone or together. Figure 7.5 shows the relationship between the result of a risk assessment (shown as either a high risk or low risk of the undesirable event occurring) and the actual outcome. When a risk assessment identifies high risk this could either be correct (a true positive) or incorrect (a false positive). When a risk assessment identifies low risk, this could either be correct (a true negative) or incorrect (false negative). Although the existence of false negatives is likely to come to light and be the subject of much concern, false positives can be more problematic as it may never be known whether the danger would have occurred if evasive action had not been taken. If the foster home in the example was assessed to be at high risk of breaking down abruptly, and as a result Zena was moved, it would never be known for sure whether in fact it would have actually broken down. Whereas if it was assessed as a low risk of breaking down abruptly, the unfolding of events would show whether this was true or false.

There are two aspects of the reliability of risk assessments: specificity (the number of false positives) and sensitivity (the number of false negatives). The two types of error have different consequences for social workers, clients and other stakeholders. If risk assessment is not specific enough to identify only those truly in danger as *high risk*, many clients and others will be subjected to unnecessary intervention and labelling, but from the position of the agency false positives are harms successfully prevented as it can never be known which cases actually fall into this group. On the other hand, if risk assessment is not sensitive enough to identify only those truly *not* in danger, as *low risk*, many high-risk situations will be missed, with disastrous results for both clients, social workers and others. Bryony Moore states that it is little wonder that many professionals err on the side of caution, with false positives being considered unofficially acceptable (Moore, 1996, p. 11). The reliability of risk assessment will partly depend on the base rate of the danger in the population being considered. Risk assessment schedules and checklists are developed in relation to high-profile low-incident harmful behaviours – for example, suicide, child abuse and violence to others, which tend to have low base rates even in groups known to be vulnerable. For example, Mark, Williams and Pollock quote a study of 1,000 parasuicides in which only 10 went on to kill themselves over the next year (Mark, Williams and Pollock, 1993, p. 14). Low base rates make specificity a particular problem, with risk assessment giving very large numbers of false positives compared with true positives (see Mark, Williams and Pollock, 1993, p. 13 in relation to suicide).

The fairness of risk

Whether to take a risk may hinge around the issue of risk accept-ability, which Brearley defined as 'whether the benefits of a course of action are such that the risks can be borne' (Brearley, 1982, p. 23). Decision makers also need to decide on the fairness of the risk defined as 'how far actions taken by one or more people are likely to impose the possibility of loss on others and therefore with how far such actions are to be taken or avoided' (Brearley, 1982, p. 23). Risk fairness recognises that risks are not taken in social isolation and one person's risk taking can be another person's hazard, as when a potentially violent person is discharged from psychiatric hospital. In the present cultural climate 'the political pressure is not explicitly against taking risks, but against exposing others to risks' (Douglas, 1992, p. 15). Zena's placement continuing to a point where the pressure was such that the foster parents' relationship broke down, could have been identified as a danger in the *staying in foster home* option. When considering an option that exposes others to the chance of a loss, a careful balance needs to be struck between the opportunities and the risks that course of action offers.

Stakeholders exposed to a chance of loss need to be consulted, so that the multifaceted nature of social situations can be fully taken into account and important aspects of and perspectives on the decision situation will not be missed. One difficulty with such consultations is the different stakeholders may have different attitudes towards risk taking and some will have more power than others to determine the decision result, an issue discussed in Chapter 3. Some stakeholders may be *risk averse* and in danger of taking an overcautious approach in which the issue of safety dominates, while others can be *risk seeking* and may veer towards recklessness. The differing positions will somehow need to be reconciled if the action taken is to have a wide level of support – but basing the choice of options on what the consequences of the decision will be is not the only way of deciding between options.

Options as Right or Wrong

The second way of choosing an option to be discussed is related to deontological ethics as opposed to the utilitarian ethics of the outcome approach (Horne, 1987, p. 31; Reamer, 1995, p. 52). There is a view that a utilitarian approach is not enough by itself and moral principles are also needed to guide actions (Bamford, 1989, p. 143). A deontological approach involves ethical reasoning about the rightness of an option in itself, without regard to its consequences, but it needs to be stressed that both approaches are ethical but based on different sets of ethics. Within a deontological approach the reason for choosing an option or rejecting it is a matter of the ethics of the action rather than ethics of outcome. Many of the principles contained in professional codes of ethics (for example, see BASW, 1996) are deontological, entailing social workers doing their duty. The extent to which social workers explicitly justify courses of action on such codes may vary from country to country (Cheetham, 1989, p. 26) but the principles encapsulated can be influential. Space only permits a brief discussion of this important reason for choosing an option but in contrast to the other reasons, it has been extensively discussed elsewhere (Rhodes, 1986; Hugman and Smith, 1995; Banks, 1995; Reamer, 1995).

Ethical principles in social work

Social work is a professional activity guided by ethical principles (BASW, 1996) and there is considerable potential for these principles to influence or determine the choice of options (Banks, 1995). Some of these principles are deontological, in that they assert that social workers should choose the course of action on the basis of what is their duty or obligation. For example, the principle of self-determination gives clients the right to make their own decisions despite the consequences. Spicker (1990) argues that the principle of self-determination is circumscribed by so many provisos that it is of little use in practice, but such principles can still have considerable influence on a social worker's thinking. Even though the rightness of an option may not be the only consideration, if an option is associated with what is regarded as the right thing to do, it will have added value as an option. One reason why Margaret favoured the option of Zena remaining in her present foster home was because it was what Zena wanted to do. Margaret advocated this option within the discussions because, as a matter of principle, she believed that Zena should determine her own future. This goes considerably further than the legal duty under the Children Act 1989, to take into account the wishes and feelings of Zena when making decisions.

The deontological approach to decision making is complicated by a number of issues, not least the fact that social workers have a number of potential sources of obligation and duty – including society, their agencies, clients, profession and personal values. Codes of ethics endeavour to relate these to each other and recognise that duties and obligations can conflict giving rise to ethical dilemmas. In any given situation it is problematic and contested what a social worker's obligations and duties are and they may need to be arranged in a hierarchical order. For example, Reamer (1995, p. 60) states that

> rules against basic harms to the necessary preconditions of human action (such as life itself, health, food, shelter, mental equilibrium) take precedence over rules against harms such as lying or revealing confidential information or threats to additive good such as recreation, education.

A deontological approach involves analysing the decision situation in terms of obligations and duties involved. This may lead to an option being clearly identified as the right course of action to follow or a clarification of the nature of the dilemma being faced, but there is no definitive list of ethical rules and processes to follow that would each time produce the morally right thing to do.

A deontological approach and an outcome approach do not necessarily give different decision making results since an option chosen as the right thing to do could also be the option chosen for its expected beneficial outcome. Likewise it is possible that an option rejected as wrong in itself may also be rejected on the basis of its considered undesirable outcome. Placing Zena with white foster parents or a children's residential centre with an all-white staff may have been rejected as a matter of deontological principle, but also considered to have a likely bad outcome. Focusing solely on the rightness of the course of action becomes a distinctive approach when an option is chosen even when the probable outcome is unwelcome. Sarah Banks gives the example of a worker deciding to honour the principles of confidentiality and self-determination rather than try and prevent the suicide of a young person (Banks, 1995, p. 152). Another example is leaving a young black person languishing in an inappropriate placement because, as a matter of ethical principle, it is not considered appropriate to place him with skilled white foster parents who are able to offer him a home.

Conflict between deontological and outcome approaches

At times there can be a conflict between pursuing a deontological principle and a good outcome which may give rise to ethical dilemmas of a kind common in social work (Rhodes, 1986). If Zena wanted to go back onto the streets, Margaret would have experienced a conflict between Zena's considered right to make her own decisions and a social worker's responsibility to promote the welfare of the client. In this instance the conflict between a deontological approach and an outcome approach, takes the form of a conflict between client autonomy and professional paternalism (Abramson, 1985). The principle of self-determination often includes a client's right to engage in self-destructive behaviour, as long as they are making an informed choice and not harming others. Margaret contemplates whether Zena's situation is one in which paternalism is justified (Gert and Culver, 1979); her conclusion is likely to hinge on whether Zena's choice is considered informed, given her age, understanding and life experience. The social worker's duty to promote the welfare of young people and doing what is in their best interests, is likely to take precedence over any commitment to the principle of self-determination, not least because the former is a legal duty. If Zena was older this may not have been the case, because adults can be regarded as having the right to make their own decisions about their lives and their own bodies even if this puts them in danger or goes against what is considered their own interests (see Chapter 3).

The Emotional Charge of an Option

The emphasis so far has been the different ethical basis of decision making and the reasoning behind a choice of options. Decision makers also need to be aware that emotions are an inextricable and important part of making a choice. From the discussion in Chapter 5, it can be expected that emotions may provide the motivation to carefully consider the options and provide important information as to how the options are being currently appraised. However, emotions can also distort a systematic consideration of courses of action when they are acted upon in inappropriate ways.

Emotions in choosing

The prospect of having to choose an option can potentially trigger emotions within the decision makers that impact on the way they think about the options. Margaret has worked closely with Zena's foster parents over the years and has grown to admire them. The prospect of possibly having to move Zena triggers a feeling of disappointment and of being let down. As discussed in Chapter 5 the usual dichotomy between sentiment and reason is misplaced since emotions give important information about how the situation is currently being appraised, with the possibility that it needs to be reappraised or the action tendency of the emotion resisted. There are contradictory expectations on social workers as regards emotions with them being expected to have neither excessive emotional involvement or under-emotional involvement (Butrym, 1976, p. 51). On the one hand emotions are regarded as unfortunate and in need of control, with social workers able to make hard choices dispassionately. On the other hand social workers are required to be sensitive and compassionate, with much value placed upon a social worker's ability to have empathy with clients.

Clients are generally recognised as being emotionally involved in the decision situation but a common error is not to take this fully into account when considering client decision making. Inexperienced social workers may expect clients to take decisions in isolation from the strong emotions they feel – for example, expecting a parent, with a strong emotional attachment to their child, to concede that they are neglecting them; or expecting an older person with a strong emotional attachment to their home to accept that they can no longer cope; or expecting a woman to leave her violent partner without appreciating the mixed emotions and feelings she experiences. Emotions have an impact on the choices people make and this needs to be recognised and taken account of when making decisions. The emotional charge of an option can be an important influence on which option is chosen, with a danger of an option being favoured solely because it was positively emotionally charged or, alternatively, rejected because it had a negative emotional charge.

Negative emotional charge

Decision makers may regard some options as having a negative emotional charge, which can take the form of a strong repelling force. An important source of negative emotional charge in social work is the fear of being a victim of violence (Norris, 1990; Brown, Bute and Ford, 1986). Options associated with such a fear can be rejected in favour of an option perceived to be more personally safe. While the emotions triggered provide important information that may need to be acted upon – for example, taking certain precautions – they are unlikely to be an appropriate reason for rejecting the option. An option can also be too emotionally painful for the decision maker to consider, for example, being reluctant to set in motion the procedures to remove children from their parents, even though their development is being severely impaired or when the decision maker overidentifies with the person's situation, as when a social worker who himself is a father does not consider the option of restricting contact between an abusing father and his son. Again the emotion is providing the decision maker with important information by signalling there is a lot at stake, which can appropriately motivate the decision makers to take due care, but should not be the reason for avoiding difficult choices.

Some options are stressful or even dangerous to implement and the prospect of a difficult implementation can give an option a strong negative emotional charge. This can both have a positive and negative impact on making choices. Such decisions usually involve drastic actions of some kind – for example, the removal of children from their parents or the compulsory admission of a person to psychiatric hospital. The prospect of a difficult implementation provides a strong incentive for decision makers to think carefully about whether such actions are fully justified, but there can also be a tendency to deny their necessity in order to avoid the trauma involved. The prospect of implementation can have a different impact on those decision makers who have a direct responsibility of implementing the decision, compared with those who do not. Those not involved in implementation may not give enough weight to the traumatic impact implementation of the decision will have, while those who have the responsibility may give too much weight.

Positive emotional charge

As well as being emotionally repelled from an option, a decision maker can be emotionally attracted or drawn to an option. The more pleasant emotions of happiness, joy, pride, love, affection and relief can attract decision makers to an option. The option of Zena staying with her foster parents has a strong positive emotional charge for Margaret, who has put considerable investment in the placement. Its success would give her a great sense of achievement. A positive emotional charge can take the form of an option offering emotional satisfaction of some need or an emotional affinity with the decision maker. For example, a social worker who has built up a relationship with a set of parents who have a learning difficulty may allow themselves to lose sight of the needs of their child. Many people go into social work out of an acute sense of social injustice and the desire to help people, but soon realise that social work is a lot more complex and may offer little job satisfaction. Feeling the need for positive feedback or wanting to please people can mean that an option can seem more attractive than it otherwise would. A strong desire to rescue children or protect older people or wanting to solve people's problems for them can attract the decision maker to an option that satisfies these needs irrespective of its merit on other counts.

Multiple reasons for choosing an option

The reasons for choosing an option have been largely treated as separate, but clearly a consideration of the likely outcomes alongside one's duty and emotions can take place simultaneously with each interacting with the other. This can be true when a particular individual decision maker may be simultaneously influenced by what is likely to give a good outcome, what is the right thing to do and their emotional response to the options. Also within any particular decision making situation each party may be influenced by a different factor. Zena's father is mostly influenced by his strong feeling of shame, Zena by fear of her father's reaction if she returned home. Her foster parents wanted what was best for Zena and so were mainly interested in the possible outcomes of the options and which was most likely to have a good outcome. An important consideration of Margaret was the principle of self-determination with Zena deciding for herself, but this was in the context of the overarching principle of promoting Zena's welfare and so ultimately she was most concerned with the possible outcomes of the options.

CHAPTER SUMMARY AND KEY POINTS

A careful and systematic consideration of the options is an important part of sound decision making. Each option needs to be appraised, with decision makers being critically aware of the various influences on making a choice and clear about what they are basing their choice on. Three ways of making a choice were identified – choosing the option that is thought most likely to give the best chance of a good outcome, the one that upholds a deontological principle or responding to the emotional charge of the options.

When making a choice of option, the following points need to be considered:

- the possible outcomes in terms of what they are and their relative likelihood and value;
- any points of deontological principle that need to be taken into account alongside or instead of the possible outcomes;
- the role emotions are playing in the choice.

Issues and tensions when making a choice include:

- the differing perspectives amongst the stakeholders as to what would be a good outcome;
- what to do when there is a clash of ethical principles;
- achieving a balance between being sensitive to the emotions involved while not acting inappropriately on them.

8

Evaluating Decisions

Decision evaluation, the last ingredient in the decision making framework, is a complex subject, with a distinction being drawn between evaluating the soundness of *decision making,* the viability of *decision implementation* and the effectiveness of *decision outcome.* Stakeholders may have different values and perspectives on decision evaluation and this chapter endeavours to clarify some of the issues and problems involved and the implications these have for social work practice. It is not possible or desirable to specifically evaluate all decisions made throughout the social work process, within assessment, planning, plan implementation and review but certain critical, difficult, sensitive or particularly consequential decisions will need to be fully evaluated. Who evaluates decisions can be a source of tension, as all stakeholders have a potential role, with the possibility that it will be carried out on a collaborative basis.

ILLUSTRATIVE EXAMPLE

Edward is an approved social worker under the Mental Health Act 1983. Six weeks ago he undertook two assessments for possible compulsory admission to psychiatric hospital under Section 2 of the Act for a period of in-patient observation. The assessments concerned two isolated young men living alone, a Mr Lake and a Mr Griffin, in respect of whom Edward decided that detention in a hospital was not the most appropriate way of providing care and treatment. The mental health team had been contacted by Mr Lake's landlord, who felt he was behaving strangely, and by Mr Griffin's neighbour, who knew he had been depressed and had not seen him for a number of days. Edward's decisions were taken in the context of two doctors having made recommendations that both men needed to be compulsorily detained in hospital in the interests of their

153

own health. Although very similar situations, the decisions had very different outcomes.

Mr Lake was found dead in his bedsit ten days later, lying on his bed with an empty bottle of pills on the bedside table, while Mr Griffin six weeks later had come out of himself and was out and about. Edward regarded both decisions as difficult, but it was not until he learnt of Mr Lake's death that he started to evaluate them. Decisions that are perceived to have bad outcomes can generate considerable concern and stakeholders may wish or demand to evaluate a decision which may be the subject of an internal or external enquiry. Potentially interested parties in Edward's decisions are his agency's management, other agencies and professionals, mental health pressure groups, the people that knew Mr Lake, his neighbours, the local press, the Mental Health Commission, professional bodies, any committee of enquiry that was set up and academic researchers. Not all stakeholders will have equal access to resources to carry out decision evaluation and part of decision evaluation practice needs to be the empowerment and involvement of clients in the evaluation of decisions that have influenced their lives.

Evaluating the Making of a Decision

Edward is particularly concerned about whether his decisions were sound, but recognises that what precisely should be included in a criteria of soundness is a matter of debate. This book has given six aspects of soundness: taking into account the contexts, promoting client involvement, consulting with the stakeholders, clear thinking about the decision situation, careful framing of the decision situation and a systematic appraisal of the options. These can be used to form a set of criteria for a sound decision, while recognising that what a sound decision is will remain a problematic and contested area. The six aspects together form a malleable, rather than rigid, framework that gives headings under which a decision's soundness can be considered.

The place of decision making evaluation in social work practice

Ideally the evaluation of the soundness of decision making would take place soon after the decision was made and would be a routine part of social work practice, both at the level of the individual practitioner and the agency. This would form part of practitioner reflective practice and agency quality assurance, with the purpose of providing feedback so that practice and agency policy could be modified or changed. Unfortunately the evaluation of the soundness of a decision will often only be prompted by things going wrong, leading to an error-driven approach to improving services and practice (Adams, 1998, p. 114), rather than a success-driven approach. Waiting for mistakes to occur means that the decision will be in the midst of being implemented or has already had a bad outcome. The perspective of *decision making* evaluation needs to be what the average skilled practitioner would have done, given what was known and what could reasonably be expected to have been known at the time, without the benefits of hindsight. Yet the circumstances of decision evaluation can often mean that it is hard to recreate how the decision situation looked at the time it was taken.

Criteria for a sound decision

There may be a measure of agreement about the six aspects of a sound decision discussed in Chapters 2 to 7 but this is likely to fall away when working out what these are to mean in practice and the related question of how they are to be measured. The six aspects are not discrete entities that are either present or absent, but multi-faceted areas that may be present in some respects but absent in others, while what indicates their absence or presence is a matter of contention. This means the degree to which each criterion needs to be met for the decision to be judged as sound, will always be problematic and a matter of judgement. Edward and his supervisor decide that the decisions should be discussed and evaluated in group supervision. The role of supervision, although supportive, involves providing a scrutinising critical ear as self-deception is always a danger (Payne, 1994, p. 49). To evaluate the decision making, the team work through the following questions together. Space only permits an indication of what they considered under each question in respect of Mr Lake's situation and the corresponding chapter number is given, that sets out in detail what is involved.

When making the decision, did Edward:

- take into account the different contexts (Chapter 2)?
- empower the client to be involved to the highest feasible level (Chapter 3)?

- consult with the stakeholders (Chapter 4)?
- clearly think about the decision situation (Chapter 5)?
- frame the decision situation without distortion (Chapter 6)?
- base his choice of action on a clear and systematic appraisal of the options (Chapter 7)?

Taking into account the different contexts

The team's discussion of the contexts that Edward needed to take into account included, the constraints and opportunities of law, regulations, official guidance, agency policy and agency procedures. Edward had consulted the Mental Health Act 1983, Code of Practice, while he was making the decision, particularly chapter 2 concerning assessment prior to possible admission under the Act (Department of Health and Welsh Office, 1993). His colleagues were interested in whether Edward's practice was consistent with the code and whether he carried out his duty. After discussion, both Edward and his colleagues were satisfied that he had sufficiently taken into account the different aspects, but recognised that unsound decisions can often be traced back to decision makers losing sight of their prime consideration. Another context they considered were the tensions between the psychiatrists and the community mental health team, which partly stemmed from the different approaches they took to mental health problems (Sheppard, 1990, p. 131). The team discussed whether the competitive atmosphere that was at times engendered negatively impinged on how Edward had made his decisions.

Empowering the client to be involved to the highest feasible level

Edward identified the level of involvement of Mr Lake as *being consulted* and had done all he could to enable him to give his point of view, listened to what he had to say and took this into account when making the decision. Mr Lake's view was that he did not need to be in hospital, that he was perfectly all right and just needed to be left alone. Edward placed much importance on the fact that Mr Lake agreed to co-operate with home treatment and his team queried whether Edward gave too much sway to Mr Lake's point of view. So much so, that it could be seen as a negotiated decision made in partnership with Mr Lake, the two of them having reached an agreement, that if Mr Lake co-operated with home treatment Edward would not make the application. Edward was satisfied that he was not unduly swayed by Mr Lake and that he made an independent judgement taking into account Mr Lake's views.

Consulting with the stakeholders

Edward, the two doctors and the community nurse had consulted with each other, Edward asking the community nurse particularly about the appropriateness and feasibility of the community-based care plan. Edward was clear that the level of involvement of the doctors was one of consultation, they having already made their decisions concerning the medical recommendations and that the decision about application was his to make independently taking into account all the circumstances. The team was concerned about the way such consultations can take place, being more of snatched conversations than considered discussion, believing more effort could have been made to reach a consensus if they had all met together. Edward felt that this was unrealistic given the pressures they were all under. He considered that in the circumstances the consultations had been as thorough as was practicable and that the important point was that they had shared the appropriate information with each other and he was aware of the full picture.

Thinking clearly about the decision situation

Edward was an experienced member of the team and had thought carefully about the decision situation. The decision was made on the basis of an analysis of the situation, using his professional intuition within the analysis to fill in the gaps. He had not been complacent about the decision, believing there were risks involved in both the home treatment plan and hospital admission. There were no impediments to vigilant information processing, being motivated by his internal conflict, having *hope* that a satisfactory solution could be found and *time* to think through the situation. The team agreed that Edward had thought about the decision situation in a careful and systematic manner and that he was clear about the issues involved. He had not allowed any misplaced sentiment to cloud his thinking and was aware of the emotions involved – particularly in relation to the prospect of a difficult admission given that Mr Lake was likely to physically resist.

Framing the decision situation without distortion

The team considered whether, in the context of time restraints, Edward had collected all the appropriate information that was available. Edward had interviewed Mr Lake and listened carefully to what he had to say. There were no known relatives to consult or previous contacts with mental health services. Mr Lake had said that he had no friends and kept himself to himself. He had only occupied the room for two months and was vague about his previous residence. The only specific comment made by the land-lord was that Mr Lake stared at him 'in a scary way'. Edward felt that in the circumstances he had collected as much information as was practicable. Edward believed that his picture of the situation had taken into account all the factors listed in the Code of Practice. He placed more weight on some factors as opposed to others. For example, more weight was placed on 'the patient's wishes and view of his own needs' than 'the nature of the illness/behaviour disorder' (Department of Health and Welsh Office, 1993, pp. 4–5). The supervisor questioned whether Edward took sufficiently into ac-count Mr Lake's isolation and his uncertain history. Edward believed at the time that there was no indication that Mr Lake was suicidal, only that he was a lonely and private person. When Edward had turned the interview to the subject of suicide, Mr Lake gave no hint of having any thoughts of ending his life. He was aware that statistically Mr Lake was a member of a high-risk group for suicide, being a young unemployed male living apart from his family, but in the absence of other factors this alone was of no predictive value. As far as was known, Mr Lake had not recently experienced any major life events entailing loss nor had he expressed any suicidal thoughts.

Edward was clear that his shorter-term goal was to enable Mr Lake to receive the care and treatment that he needed in the least restricted context as practicable and his longer-term goal was to promote Mr Lake's mental well-being. His supervisor agreed with the appropriateness of these goals, but emphasised neither of them were achieved. Edward had identified the options as compulsory admission to hospital or Mr Lake receiving treatment and care in his own home. Framing the decision situation as consisting of these two options was considered appropriate, given Mr Lake's psycho-logical state, his refusal of voluntary admission and the need for some psychiatric intervention. The feasibility of each option was considered, with the community-based care plan having been worked out with the other members of the community mental health team. This involved a weekly visit to Mr Lake by the community nurse and attendance at a day centre. The team wondered whether the feasibility of the remaining at home option had been sufficiently thought through – particularly the speed at which the care plan could be put fully into action but on the whole his frame of the situation was believed to be well reasoned and consistent with the available information.

Basing the choice of action on a clear and systematic appraisal of the options

Edward had systematically appraised each option in terms of the value and likelihood of its possible outcomes, with the home treatment option on balance being judged to be the one most likely to give a good outcome. Edward explained his analysis to the team, who wondered whether the outcome of the decision had been Edward's main concern or whether the deontological principle of self-determination had been the deciding factor. Another team member felt that a clearer focus on the risk involved in the home treatment option may have been appropriate. Edward explained that he believed that the hospital admission option was equally fraught with risk for Mr Lake, though it may have been a safer option from Edward's career point of view. The supervisor also questioned whether the prospect of forcibly getting Mr Lake to hospital had an undue influence on Edward. The emotions triggered by the prospect of a difficult admission gave a strong incentive to carefully consider the options but had Edward been emotionally repelled from the admission option and attracted to the community option?

Only a brief sketch has been given of the team's discussion, but on balance they came to the conclusion that Edward's decision had been sound at the time it was taken but later proved not to be effective. This did not stop Edward regretting the way things had turned out and the part he had played or there being differing perspectives on his decision. For example, the consultant psychiatrist was not of the same opinion, believing that Mr Lake was ill and in need of hospital treatment and that it was the illness itself that prevented Mr Lake having insight into this. She felt that Edward was far too concerned about Mr Lake's wishes and the detrimental effects of being compulsorily admitted and that, by contrast, he was too optimistic about the ability of the mental health team to monitor such situations and effectively implement a community-based care plan.

Evaluating Decision Implementation

Having decided on balance that Edward's decision was a sound one, the team turned to the evaluation of its implementation. Decision framing is concerned with whether the options are feasible, while decision implementation evaluation is concerned with whether the chosen option proved to be viable. It is beyond the scope of this book to discuss decision implementation and monitoring in detail, but clearly it is a factor that needs to be taken into account when evaluating a decision. Whether a decision was successfully implemented reflects on the soundness of the decision and in turn will impact on its outcome. Decision situations will drift or deteriorate, if implementation problems are not picked up by monitoring and rectified. The discussion here will be limited to three questions: what is the place of decision implementation evaluation in social work practice, was the implementation monitored, and was the decision fully implemented?

What is the place of decision implementation evaluation in social work practice?

The evaluation of decision implementation ideally takes place at a point in time that allows the consideration of how the plan is working out in practice, but can be prompted by things going wrong, feedback from monitoring or a complaint. Depending on the nature of the plan, decision implementation may be evaluated at different intervals of time – for example, six weeks, three months or six months intervals, when it may form part of a more general review. A review had been planned in Mr Lake's case to take place in six weeks time and the fact that Mr Lake died before the review took place demonstrates the importance of routine ongoing reflective practice and the monitoring of situations between reviews. There is a danger that reviews can become set pieces that do not systematically consider whether previous decisions have been fully and successfully implemented. When such short-termism prevails, the situation is looked at afresh at each review rather than from the perspective of whether previous decisions have been successfully implemented and remain appropriate.

Was the implementation of the decision monitored?

Decision implementation needs to be monitored because new information can come to light, the decision situation may change or implementation problems may develop. The existence of a reactive style of practice, that requires external pressure to prompt action, can mean decision implementation is given scant attention unless there is a crisis. What is needed is a proactive style of practice that is self-motivating, with it being clear whose role it is to monitor the implementation and how and when monitoring is to take place. When decision implementers remain confident that the decision was a sound one, it would be inappropriate to change course at the first sign of trouble. Nevertheless when feedback from monitoring indicates that implementation is going wrong, plans will need to be modified or changed accordingly. The community nurse who was identified as the key worker with the role of monitoring Mr Lake's care plan had made one visit to Mr Lake before his death. The case notes showed that Mr Lake had been co-operative in discussing his situation and how he was feeling. When the community nurse had discussed suicidal intent with him, Mr Lake had given no suggestion of having any thoughts of ending his own life.

Was the decision fully implemented?

The decision Edward made that day involved a plan to provide the care and treatment Mr Lake needed while remaining at home. A pertinent question to ask, in the evaluation of Edward's decision, is whether the plan was fully and appropriately implemented. When things go wrong the failure may have been in the implementation of the decision, rather than in the making of the decision. Sometimes decisions are not implemented – for example, decisions taken at reviews may not be acted upon but more usually it is a question of whether a decision was fully implemented in the spirit in which it was made. Plans can be partially implemented or shoddily implemented or over a period of time be allowed to lapse, particularly when there are other, more immediately pressing matters to deal with. In a number of ways the success or otherwise of implementing a decision is related to the soundness of decision making. For example, the degree of commitment of those implementing the decision will be influenced by how far they participated in the decision making. In addition, an ill-thought-through decision will run into implementation difficulties and may be soon abandoned or even worse pursued with possibly dire consequences.

Evaluating Decision Outcome

The concern here is with the evaluation of the *actual* outcomes that occur after the decision has been implemented, while the previous chapter considered the *possible* outcomes of the option within the decision frame. The purpose of sound decision making is to bring about favourable outcomes; whether these are achieved is an important focus of decision evaluation. While there is much to be learnt from tracing and evaluating the outcomes of decisions this also raises a number of questions and this section will discuss the following issues: what is the place of outcome evaluation in social work practice, what is a decision outcome, when does a decision have an outcome, how are decision outcomes to be measured and what value is to be placed on an outcome?

What is the place of outcome evaluation in social work practice?

The outcomes of decisions need to have a central place in decision evaluation, so as to provide feedback by which professional practice can be developed. The fact that the outcome is unknown at the time a decision is made and implemented has important implications; but these should not detract from the ultimate importance of decision outcome. The effectiveness of a decision in achieving its goal will remain unknown unless its outcome is evaluated but there can be formidable barriers to tracing decision outcomes including staff attitudes, lengthy time-scales, methodological issues and limited resources. A much longer-term and systematic perspective is needed than is often in evidence, if decision outcome evaluation is to become a routine part of reflective practice, professional super-vision, quality assurance and decision research.

What is a decision outcome?

Decision outcomes will be defined as the consequences that follow decision implementation in relation to the decision goals. The focus is on what Cheetham, Fuller, McIvor and Petch (1992) refer to as client-based outcomes as opposed to service-based outcomes. The outcome of Edward's decision, not to make an application for Mr Lake's admission, is likely to be regarded as Mr Lake's suicide. The presence or absence of a life event like death, is only one of a number of ways the occurrence of decision outcomes can be marked but this will be used to consider what is meant by the term. Life events are not outcomes in themselves, but àre identified as such by decision evaluators and can be matters of contention and debate. A life event is a happening that impacts on a person's life, such as getting married, moving house, the birth of a child or death of a parent. Decision goals may involve the achievement of certain life events – for example, moving to independent living – with the occurrence of that life event being a good outcome and its non-occurrence a bad outcome. Avoidance of a life event may also be a decision goal, for example, entering residential care, with its non-occurrence regarded as a good outcome and its occurrence a bad outcome.

Saying Mr Lake's death is the outcome of Edward's decision does not mean that Edward is responsible for Mr Lake's suicide or that he caused Mr Lake's suicide. Rather it means that it was regarded as part of his role to prevent Mr Lake's suicide and to promote his mental health and safety. There is no direct causal relationship between what happened to Mr Lake and the decision taken by Edward. Regarding Mr Lake's death as the outcome of Edward's decision, relates to Edward's goal in making the decision and the responsibility he carried for promoting Mr Lake's mental well-being. As previously stated the absence or occurrence of a life event is only one way of evaluating the outcome of a decision. The outcome of the decision in respect of Mr Griffin is more likely to have been conceived in terms of his state of being some time after the decision had been taken, an issue to be discussed in the next section.

When does a decision have an outcome?

Only a minority of decision situations come to an end, in the way that Mr Lake's did, when a life event clearly identifies the outcome of the decision. More common is Mr Griffin's situation where there is a problem about when the outcome of a decision is seen to be occurring. There is a need for evaluation of decision outcomes to become a routine part of practice but when no clear-cut event presents itself as an outcome, the notion of decision outcome may only come into play if somebody or some system prompts it. This prompting, if it happens at all, is likely to be done by reflective practice, professional supervision, practice audit, a quality assurance scheme or research. The absence of a clearly definable event means a convenient but more or less arbitrary time interval needs to be identified when the outcome can be gauged. This involves following up situations after a certain period of time, possibly before, at or after agency contact with the client has ceased.

Whatever time interval is chosen there is always the possibility that it is too soon to gauge the 'final' outcome or too late to capture valuable short-lived effects. Within the continuity of life the notion of 'final' outcome is problematic, with decision outcomes being a social construction rather than discoverable fact. Edward's group supervision session is taking place six weeks after he took the decision in respect of Mr Griffin. The team may evaluate the outcome as good at the time, but next week things could take a drastic turn for the worse, placing the decision in a different light. Six weeks may be regarded as too soon, with six months or twelve months being seen as more realistic and as with others matters the client's perspective on the appropriate time to gauge the decision outcome should be an important influence. In their outcome research on child protection decisions, Farmer and Owen (1995) chose twenty months as an appropriate period after which to assess outcomes. This may be considered a relatively short time in relation to a child growing into an adult, but even following up situations at this modest interval caused considerable methodological, resource and practical problems. Many decisions in social work have even longer-term considerations. For example, the decision to place a child for adoption with a particular family can only be effectively evaluated in terms of outcome decades after it is made.

How are decision outcomes to be measured?

When outcomes are measured in terms of the absence or occurrence of a life event within a specified time period, their measurement is relatively straightforward but usually it is not sufficient to solely measure outcomes in this way. Edward's decision in respect of Mr Griffin is unlikely to be evaluated as having a good outcome just because he was alive six weeks later. The outcome will more probably be related to whether the longer-term decision goals – of promoting his well-being, quality of life or life satisfaction – have been achieved. These are examples of evaluative dimensions that were discussed in Chapter 7 in relation to the value of possible outcomes and what constitutes human well-being, quality of life and life satisfaction are matters of contention, often being defined by different people in different ways (Seed and Lloyd, 1997, p. 4). Edward had a long discussion with Mr Griffin before group supervision about his well-being, quality of life and life satisfaction compared with the period before Edward decided not to apply for compulsory admission to hospital. The process of translating decision goals into measurable outcomes is conceptually and operationally problematic. It includes whether outcomes are to be considered as subjective states or observable facts or a combination of both. Finding out if clients' lives have certain qualities can either be done by listening to clients' beliefs and feelings about the existence of that quality in their lives or by using external observational measures, such as, frequency of contact with other people or how often the client goes out (Nocon and Qureshi, 1996, p. 10). An issue is whether clients define what constitutes human well-being, quality of life or life satisfaction in the context of their own lives or whether professionals and experts do it for them.

A number of ready-made measurement instruments exist (see, for example, Oliver, 1991; Greenley, Greenberg and Brown, 1997) that provide standard measures of well-being, quality of life and life satisfaction. These usually are in the form of questionnaires, but their validity, reliability and usefulness in day-to-day practice can be questioned. They do enable some attempt to be made to measure outcome in a systematic way (see Bowling, 1991) but in their discussion of outcomes of community care Nocon and Qureshi conclude that 'there is no off-the-shelf solution to the question of outcome measurement' (Nocon and Qureshi, 1996, p. 135). The issue is whether practitioners should use standardised measures, many of which were developed for a different purpose or whether social workers and clients should devise situation-specific ways of measuring outcomes in relation to their chosen evaluative dimensions in the context of their own aspirations. On the one hand decision outcome evaluation can be considered as a necessary part of routine professional practice that is responsive to the unique features of decision situations. On the other hand if decision outcomes were measured in a standardised way within or across agencies, data could more easily be aggregated and used to inform changes in policy, services and practice. It is beyond the scope of this chapter to consider these issues of outcome measurement in depth and the reader is referred to a wide variety of literature (see, for example, Cheetham, Fuller, McIvor and Petch, 1992; Parker, Ward, Jackson, Aldgate and Wedge, 1991, chapter 2; Wright, Haycox and Leedham, 1994, pp. 52–103; Nocon and Qureshi, 1996).

What value to place on the outcome?

The issues discussed in the previous chapter in relation to the use of *good* and *bad* to place a value on *possible* outcomes, apply equally to the evaluation of *actual* outcomes. In many situations what is a good outcome for one stakeholder is a bad outcome for other stakeholders. This raises the questions of good outcome or bad outcome for whom and whether central place is given to the client's perspective as to whether an outcome is good or bad. Agreement and disagreement between social workers, clients and other stakeholders about decision goals will tend to be reflected in agreement and disagreement about decision outcomes. Both Edward and Mr Griffin regarded his staying out of hospital, continuing to co-operate with community treatment and making steady progress as a good outcome, although they placed different emphasis on his co-operation with treatment. Edward and his colleagues regarded Mr Lake's death as a bad outcome, while Mr Lake's perspective on his death is unknowable.

Being a good or bad outcome is not a property of a particular life event or state of being – for example, moving to residential care (when considered as an outcome) is not inevitably good or bad. The value of an outcome is a matter of judgement which may differ between stakeholders, between decision situations and between different points of time within decision situations. Agreement about the value of some outcomes (for example, there is likely to be agreement that Mr Lake's death was a bad outcome) should not detract from the problematic nature of giving an outcome a value.

Some may hold, what may be regarded as a minority opinion, that Mr Lake's suicide was a good outcome, if he truly intended to die having made a fully considered and informed decision with a balanced mind. Within this view Mr Lake is regarded as an autonomous person with the right to take his own life and any paternalistic attempts to stop him would have been unjustified (Fairbairn, 1995, p. 166). In many situations whether an outcome is actually good or bad is a matter of contention. For example, in Chapter 5 Mr Smith decides to return home against medical advice and enjoys his own home for six months before he dies in his sleep one night, to be found by his home help the next morning. This is likely to be regarded as a good outcome, but views are likely to differ if he was found by the home help, on a Monday morning, lying on the floor in a half-conscious state having been there since Friday evening.

Decision Making and Decision Outcome

The discussion now turns to the problematic relationship between decision making processes and decision outcomes. For the sake of clarity, decision making can be regarded as sound or unsound and outcomes regarded as good or bad. Even though this is a simplification it will help identify the issues in the relationship between decision making and decision outcomes, the four possibilities being shown in Figure 8.1 below. A *sound decision* may have a *good outcome* and be regarded as an *effective decision* or a *bad outcome*

FIGURE 8.1   *The relationship between decision making and decision outcome*

		decision making	
		sound	**unsound**
decision outcome	**good**	effective decision	good fortune
	bad	bad fortune	culpable decision

and be regarded as *bad fortune*. An *unsound decision* can have a *good outcome* and be regarded as *good fortune* or a *bad outcome* and be regarded as a *culpable decision*. The four possibilities – of effective decision, bad fortune, good fortune and culpable decision – are discussed below.

Effective decision

Edward's sound decision in relation to Mr Griffin led to a good outcome and so could be regarded as an effective decision. These situations are a neglected aspect of decision evaluation, with emphasis being placed on decisions that produce bad outcomes. When a sound decision is linked to a good outcome, decision makers should be given some of the credit and lessons learnt about what made the decision making effective. Focus needs to be on what components of decision making link with effective outcomes, so any necessary changes can be made to the criteria for sound decisions and successful implementation – in the light of what turns out to be effective decision making. The absence of a causal link between decision making and decision outcome means that it is not possible to come up with a formula that will produce good outcomes time after time, but what is regarded as good practice in decision making and decision implementation could be improved and refined.

Bad fortune

If Edward's decision making in relation to Mr Lake is evaluated as sound and the outcome as bad, it will have been a situation of bad fortune. There has been a debate within social work as to whether decision makers can still be blamed for a bad outcome even if they made what is regarded as sound decisions. The question is whether decision makers like Edward, who having made a sound decision, can still be held accountable for the bad outcome (Macdonald, 1990; Hollis and Howe, 1987). The argument that they cannot hinges on: the validity of a definition of a sound decision; the acceptance that accountability is for the making of a sound decision; and the belief that decision outcome depends on other factors as well as decision making. Saying that decision makers who make sound decisions should not be blamed for bad outcomes does not mean that they are indifferent to the outcome or do not experience deep regret and misgivings or blame themselves for what has happened (O'Sullivan, 1988, pp. 15–16). It is to say that, given a number of factors to be discussed further in the conclusion, decision makers can only be held accountable for whether or not they made a *sound* decision.

Good fortune

Given the lack of a causal link between a decision and its outcome, it is possible for a decision that has been evaluated as unsound to be associated with an outcome that is evaluated as good. In such situations the decision makers may be regarded as lucky, having experienced considerable good fortune. The decision makers' good fortune should not detract from the issue of bad practice and any criticism, feedback, remedial action or disciplinary action should be unaffected by the good outcome. If Edward had made the decision in respect of Mr Griffin in a reckless way without due regard to the circumstances, this should become the subject of critical attention as much as if it had a bad outcome. This is unlikely to happen in practice, as it is bad outcomes that tend to trigger decision making evaluation, while good outcomes are passed over without comment.

Culpable decision

Culpable decisions are when decision makers make unsound decisions and there is a bad outcome; but who or what is culpable needs to be questioned. There will be occasions when decision makers can be blamed for unsound decision making and so the bad outcome, but it should not be automatically assumed that it is the decision makers that are culpable, there being other possible explanations. Decision makers can be reckless, negligent or incompetent, but errors of judgement can be made by otherwise careful, vigilant and competent decision makers who are operating in an environment that does not allow this competence to operate. Unsound decisions can be made by otherwise able and skilful decision makers, when they are overworked and not provided with appropriate support systems. Even when incompetence is located within the decision makers, their agencies and their society may need to share some of the responsibility, particularly in relation to the education and training made available to them.

CHAPTER SUMMARY AND KEY POINTS

The argument of this chapter was that the development of social work will be aided by the systematic evaluation of decision practice. Three aspects of a decision practice were identified as in need of evaluation – decision making, decision implementation and decision outcomes. The relationship between these three is important but problematic, with the viability of implementation and effectiveness of outcome being related to the soundness of decision making, but not in a straightforward lineal way. Sound decision making was given formative importance as it increases the chances that decision implementation will be viable and decision outcomes will be effective in achieving the decision makers' goals. The notion of decision outcome is fraught with difficulties, particularly as to when it occurs, its measurement and value. Despite these difficulties, the evaluation of decision outcomes is imperative so that the eventual effectiveness of decision making can be related back to how it was made.

When evaluating decisions the following points need to be considered:

- the soundness of the decision making;
- viability of the decision's implementation; and
- the effectiveness of the decision's outcome.

Issues and tensions when evaluating decision practice include:

- by what criteria and from whose perspective is the soundness of the decision making to be evaluated;
- how to ensure that decisions are fully implemented while responding to ongoing changes in the decision situation; and
- when are decisions to be regarded as having an outcome and from whose perspective are they to be evaluated.

9

Conclusions

This conclusion will consider the limitations on what sound decision making in social work can achieve and why it alone cannot ensure good outcomes. Decision making is just one of a number of factors that can be identified as contributing to decision outcomes; others include the nature of the society in which decision situations are located and the social positions of clients. Sound decision making can engage with these factors, but they are often beyond the direct influence of the stakeholders. Five reasons are considered in relation to why sound decision making in social work cannot ensure good outcomes, followed by a brief examination of the issue of who or what is responsibile for bad outcomes and the need to prevent them occurring.

It is not acceptable always to take the safest option

There are a number of reasons why always taking the apparently safe option would not avoid bad outcomes. What appears as the safe option may in other respects be a risky option, for example: going into care, being compulsorily detained in hospital or being admitted to a residential home all carry their own risks. If Edward had decided to make an application for compulsory admission, the outcome may not have been any different for Mr Lake, as his risk of suicide would not necessarily have been reduced by hospital admission and may have actually been increased. What would have been different is that the blame for his death would have shifted to the hospital staff. To always take the apparently safe option would mean large numbers of clients being subjected to unnecessary interference in their lives and the denial of adult rights to take risks. Edward faced the problem that it is not possible to specify who, of those in high-risk groups, will actually go on to make a

171

suicide attempt. This means decision making in social work is a matter of balance between risk and safety. If informed risks have to be taken, there will be occasions when the feared event will happen, despite sound decision making.

Competing claims within the decision situation

Another reason why sound decision making does not make inevitable a good outcome for *all* the stakeholders is that one person's good outcome can be another person's bad outcome. When there are primary and secondary clients, an increase in the quality of life of one client can be a decrease in the quality of life of another. Parents may regard their neglected children flourishing in care as a bad outcome, since it points to the inadequacies of their own parenting, but from the children's point of view it can be regarded as a good outcome. Enjoying staying in one's own home can be regarded as a good outcome, but a carer may regard the stress this puts them under as a bad outcome. Given the competing interests within decision situations in social work, sound decisions may mean that some stakeholders have a good outcome while others in the same decision situation regard it as a bad outcome.

The future cannot be predicted with certainty

As was discussed in Chapter 7, the future cannot be predicted with certainty, but it is relatively easy to backtrack from an event like Mr Lake's suicide and claim that the signs were there to see at the time the assessment was made and his suicide should have been predicted. This involves retrospective reasoning and a world in which events unfold in an ordered and predictable fashion with the presence of certain factors in the decision situation determining that it will develop in a particular way. Some situations may appear to have certain features that make particular events seem pretty much inevitable (Campbell, 1995) but, for example, there is no reliable way of predicting suicide (Mark, Williams and Pollock, 1993). An alternative view is that in the social universe, events, happenings and states of being do not follow predictable patterns and are more accurately characterised as chaos in which the future cannot be predicted with certainty. Benign or random developments in the decision situation can always turn out to have unforeseen consequences. For example, the day after the community nurse visited, Edward received a letter containing some bad news that had a profound effect on him. A careful consideration of the factors believed to increase the risk of a danger occurring is an important aspect of sound decision making but this should not be confused with the ability to accurately and reliably predict the future.

Decision making is not the only input into decision situations

Decision making is only one of many inputs into decision situations, the term *input* being used with caution in the absence of a more suitable alternative. It is borrowed from the production of welfare approach (Davies and Knapp, 1981, p. 5), but is used to refer to a broad range of antecedent factors that have potential influence on what happens in terms of the decision outcome. There is a wide variety of inputs other than decision making, each with its own impact that can contribute to the decision outcome. The inputs range from the early life experiences of Mr Lake to the nature of the society in which he lived. They include the other aspects of the agency's contact with him and that of other agencies. To simply focus on decision making as an explanation for a bad outcome, as if it was the sole input, is seriously flawed. Some inputs may be seen to have a positive influence on outcomes, while others have a negative influence, while others are so pervasive that they have an over-whelming influence. If Edward had known about Mr Lake's family history of severe emotional abuse, of which he gave no hint, his picture of the situation may have been very different. If further progress is to be made in preventing bad outcomes such negative inputs themselves need to become the focus of preventative work, at a point in time before decision situations develop.

Lack of opportunity

Clients and social workers may not have the opportunity, through lack of resources, to have the radical impact on life circumstances that is sometimes needed to have a good outcome. Life circum-stances can be constraining and lack of opportunity to bring about improvements can seriously affect the client's life chances, meaning that many of their aspirations remain beyond reach. The circum-stances of people's lives are embedded in the structures of society and within the context of these structures bad outcomes may sometimes seem inevitable. It has been argued that the aim of social work should be 'to contribute to the transformation of society' (Mullaly, 1993, p. 153), an aspiration that may appear unrealistic. Yet, if social work is serious about preventing bad outcomes, its commitment to 'bring to the attention of those in power, and of the general public, ways in which the activities of government, society or agencies create or contribute to hardship and suffering' (BASW, 1996) will need to be more forthrightly put into action. At the very least political lobbying about the effects of poverty, discrimination, oppression and lack of opportunity will need to be given more emphasis.

Who or what is responsible for bad outcomes?

It has been argued that decision makers, including social workers, from time to time make unsound decisions and when they do so, some of the responsibility for a bad outcome can be laid at their door. There can be a debate about what a sound decision consists of, but if decision makers have made a sound decision they cannot be justifiably blamed for a bad outcome. Decision evaluators – whether they are workers, clients, commissions of enquiry, the general public, the media, agency management, the government or pressure groups – often need somebody to blame. Over the years social workers have been a convenient scapegoat, drawing attention away from the problems endemic in society. It is as if there is a cultural need to explain away undesirable events by finding some-body to blame. All cultures need some way of explaining misfortune and within some societies this can take the form of finding someone already unpopular to blame (Douglas, 1992). The society we live in is 'almost ready to treat every death as chargeable to someone's account, every accident as caused by someone's criminal negligence, every sickness a threatened prosecution' (Douglas, 1992, pp. 15–16). There is a serious question about the appropriateness of finding somebody or something to blame, and a need to move beyond the issue of blame (Reder *et al.*, 1993), but the question of blame does enable an important issue to be raised.

   If the decision makers who make sound decisions are not to be blamed for bad outcomes, who or what is? It has been argued that the reasons for bad outcomes are complex, with the whole notion of cause and effect being open to question, some things being more appropriately regarded as happening without a direct cause. Many interacting factors on different levels can be implicated as playing a part in bringing about life events and states of being that are regarded as decision outcomes. These form an irreducible tangle of causes and the explanation of why things happen cannot be reduced to a single cause such as genes, personality, family dynamics or structure of society. Complexity involves a potentially unlimited number of possible relevant factors which interact in ways that make it unclear what influence they have on the unfolding events. Having said this, an attempt to disentangle the reasons for Mr Lake's death could go in a number of directions. On one level it could be said that Mr Lake having free will, chose to die, so he could take responsibility for his own death. On another level it could be argued that although people do make choices in their lives, these are always made in a context that is not entirely of their choosing. Society shapes the range and quality of options available to people, so the way society is organised and structured could, in the last analysis, be held responsible for his death.

Preventing bad outcomes

As a final comment it is necessary to return to Chapter 1 and the focus on decision making itself, which, although important, should not be allowed to draw attention away from the need for changes to be made in society. While decision makers and others can learn from evaluating decision making, decision implementation and their relationship to bad outcomes, it needs to be recognised that sound decision making alone will not eliminate bad outcomes. The focus should also be on other inputs into decision situations which may need to be targets for change. At least some bad outcomes are explained by the poor life chances of social work clients, who tend to be drawn from the bottom rungs of an unequal society. If a completely deterministic point of view is to be avoided, adult clients need to take some responsibility for bad outcomes of life decisions they make, otherwise they would be seen solely as victims rather than autonomous human beings. Nevertheless people do *not* have choice over all the circumstances of their lives, such as the social structures of oppression, that are an inheritance from the past directly encountered by them in their day-to-day lives. It is these circumstances, along with factors on other levels, that prevent sound decision making always leading to good outcomes in social work. The focus on decision making, important as it is, should not detract from the need to eradicate these circumstances. It is a responsibility of social workers alongside others to bring this to the attention of the general public, the mass media and those in government.

CHAPTER SUMMARY AND KEY POINTS

This final chapter considered why sound decision making will not always lead to a good outcome. Although sound decision making is an important ingredient in the occurrence of good outcomes, it is not sufficient in itself to ensure their occurrence. Social situations are complex with many interacting factors. This may mean that despite sound decision making bad outcomes occur.

When contemplating why bad outcomes occur, a range of factors need to be considered including:

- any risk that was integral to the decision situation no matter what course of action was taken;
- any competing claims within the decision situation that meant inevitably that some stakeholders would regard the outcome as bad; and
- whether the circumstances meant there was a lack of opportunity to achieve a good outcome.

Issues and tensions in considering why bad outcomes occur despite sound decision making include:

- the inability to predict the future with certainty;
- the difficulty of disentangling the various inputs to the decision situation and the influence they may have had on the outcome;
- learning from bad outcomes without being preoccupied by the issue of blame; and
- not letting a focus on sound decision making detract from the need to bring about changes in society.

Bibliography

Abramson, M. (1985) 'The Autonomy–Paternalism Dilemma in Social Work Practice', *Social Casework*, vol. 66, part 7, pp. 387–93.

Adams, J. (1995) *Risk* (London: UCL Press).

Adams, R. (1995) 'Truth and Love in Intermediate Treatment', *British Journal of Social Work*, vol. 15, no. 4, pp. 391–401.

Adams, R. (1996a) *The Personal Social Services: Clients, Consumers or Citizens* (London: Longman).

Adams, R. (1996b) *Social Work and Empowerment*, 2nd edn (Basingstoke: Macmillan).

Adams, R. (1998) *Quality Social Work* (Basingstoke: Macmillan).

Adams, R. and O'Sullivan, T. (1994) *Social Work with and within Groups, Unit 1: The Basics of Groups and Group Work* (Birmingham: Open Learning Foundation/BASW).

Ahmad, B. (1990) *Black Perspectives in Social Work* (Birmingham: Venture Press).

Ahmed, S. (1986) 'Cultural Racism in Work with Asian Women and Girls', in S. Ahmed, J. Cheetham and J. Small (eds), *Social Work with Black Children and their Families* (London: B. T. Batsford Ltd), pp. 140–54.

Aitken, L. and Griffin, G. (1996) *Gender Issues in Elder Abuse* (London: Sage).

Aldgate, J. (1989) *Using Written Agreement with Children and Families* (London: Family Rights Group).

Aldridge, J. and Becker, S. (1993) *Children who Care: Inside the World of Young Carers* (Leicestershire: University of Loughborough).

Aldridge, M. (1994) *Making Social Work News* (London: Routledge).

Allen, N. (1992) *Making Sense of the Children Act*, 2nd edn (Harlow: Longman).

Arnstein, S. R. (1969) 'A Ladder of Citizen Participation in the USA', *Journal of the American Institute of Planners*, vol. 35, no. 4, pp. 216–24.

Atkin, K. and Rollings, J. (1996) 'Looking after Their Own? Family Caregiving among Asian and Afro-Caribbean Communities' in W. I. U. Ahmad and K. Atkin (eds), *'Race' and Community Care* (Buckingham: Open University Press) pp. 73–86.

Bachrach, P. and Baratz, M. S. (1962) 'Two Faces of Power', *American Political Science Review*, vol. 56, pp. 937–52.

Baldwin, N. (1990) *The Power to Care in Children's Homes* (Aldershot: Avebury).

Bamford, T. (1989) 'Discretion and Managerialism' in S. Shardlow (ed.), *The Values of Change in Social Work* (London: Routledge) pp. 135–54.

Bamford, T. (1990) *The Future of Social Work* (Basingstoke: Macmillan).

Banks, S. (1995) *Ethics and Values in Social Work* (Basingstoke: Macmillan).

Barber, J. G. (1991) *Beyond Casework* (Basingstoke: Macmillan).

Barford, R. and Wattam, C. (1991) 'Children's Participation in Decision-Making', *Practice*, vol. 5, no. 2, pp. 93–102.

Barker, M. (1981) *The New Racism* (London: Junction Books).

Baron, R. S., Kerr, N. L. and Miller, N. (1992) *Group Processes, Group Decision, Group Action* (Buckingham: Open University Press).

BASW (1996) *The Code of Ethics for Social Work* (Birmingham: British Association of Social Workers).

BASW (1998) *Mental Incapacity and Decision-Making: Professional Implications for Social Workers* (Birmingham: British Association of Social Workers).

Baylor, A. L. (1997) 'A Three-Component Conception of Intuition: Immediacy, Sensing Relationships, and Reason', *New Ideas in Psychology*, vol. 15, no. 2, pp. 185–94.

Beach, L. R. (1990) *Image Theory: Decision Making in Personal and Organisational Contexts* (Chichester, England: John Wiley and Sons).

Beetham, D. (1991) *The Legitimation of Power* (Basingstoke: Macmillan).

Beresford, P. and Croft, S. (1993) *Citizen Involvement: A Practical Guide for Change* (Basingstoke: Macmillan).

Berger, P. and Luckmann, T. (1966) *The Social Construction of Reality* (Harmondsworth: Penguin Books).

Bernstein, B. (1971) 'On the Classification and Framing of Educational Knowledge', in F. D. Young (ed.), *Knowledge and Control: New Directions for the Sociology of Education* (London: Collier-Macmillan) pp.47–69.

Biggs, S. (1992) 'Groupwork and Professional Attitudes to Older Age', in K. Morgan, (ed.), *Gerontology: Responding to an Ageing Society* (London: Jessica Kingsley in association with the British Society of Gerontology) pp. 84–98.

Biggs, S., Phillipson, C. and Kingston, P. (1995) *Elder Abuse in Perspective* (Buckingham: Open University Press).

Bowling, A. (1991) *Measuring Health: A Review of Quality of Life Measurement Scales* (Milton Keynes: Open University Press).

Bradshaw, J. (1972) 'The Concept of Social Need', *New Society*, vol. 19, 30 March, pp. 640–43.

Brah, A. (1992) 'Difference, Diversity and Differentiation', in J. Donald and A. Rattansi (eds), *Race, Culture and Difference* (London: Sage) pp. 126–45.

Brandon, D. (1995) *Advocacy: Power to People with Disability* (Birmingham: Venture Press).

Brandon, M., Schofield, G. and Trinder, L. (1998) *Social Work with Children* (Basingstoke: Macmillan).

Braye, S. and Preston-Shoot, M. (1992) *Practising Social Work Law* (Basingstoke: Macmillan).

Braye, S. and Preston-Shoot, M. (1995) *Empowering Practice in Social Care* (Buckingham: Open University Press).

Brearley, C. P. (1982) *Risk and Social Work: Hazards and Helping* (London: Routledge).

Bristow, K. (1994) 'Liberation and Regulation? Some Paradoxes of Empowerment', *Critical Social Policy*, vol. 14, no. 3, pp. 34–46.

Brown, A. (1984) *Consultation: An Aid to Successful Social Work* (London: Heinemann).

Brown, A. and Bourne, I. (1996) *The Social Work Supervisor* (Buckingham: Open University Press).

Brown, H. C. (1998) *Social Work and Sexuality: Working with Lesbians and Gay Men* (Basingstoke: Macmillan).

Brown, R., Bute, S. and Ford, P. (1986) *Social Workers at Risk: The Prevention and Management of Violence* (Basingstoke: Macmillan).

Butrym, Z. T. (1976) *The Nature of Social Work* (London and Basingstoke: Macmillan).

Calder, M. C. (1995) 'Child Protection: Balancing Paternalism and Partnership', *British Journal of Social Work*, vol. 25, pp. 729–66.

Campbell, J. C. (ed.) (1995) *Assessing Dangerousness: Violence by Sexual Offenders, Batterers and Child Abusers* (Thousand Oaks: Sage).

Carroll, J. S. and Johnson, E. J. (1990) *Decision Research: A Field Guide* (London: Sage Publications).

Carson, D. (1988) 'Risk-Taking Policies', *Journal of Social Welfare Law*, vol. 5, pp. 328–32.

Challis, L. (1990) *Organising Public Social Services* (Harlow: Longman).

Cheetham, J. (1989) 'Values in Action', in S. Shardlow (ed.), *The Values of Change in Social Work* (London: Routledge) pp. 24–41.

Cheetham, J., Fuller, R., McIvor, G. and Petch, A. (1992) *Evaluating Social Work Effectiveness* (Buckingham: Open University Press).

Cicirelli, V. G. (1992) *Family Caregiving: Autonomous and Paternalistic Decision Making* (Newbury Park: Sage).

Cioffi, J. (1997) 'Heuristics, Servants to Intuition in Clinical Decision-Making', *Journal of Advanced Nursing*, vol. 26, pp. 203–208.

Clarke, J. (ed.) (1993) *A Crisis in Care? Challenges to Social Work* (London: Sage).

Clyde, J. J. (1992) *The Report of the Inquiry into the Removal of Children from Orkney in February 1991* (Edinburgh: HMSO).

Compton, B. R. and Galaway, B. (1989) *Social Work Processes*, 4th edn (Belmont:Wadsworth).

Corby, B., Millar, M. and Young, L. (1994) 'Power Play', *Community Care*, 20-26th October, p. 24.

Croft, S. and Beresford, P. (1993) *Getting Involved: A Practical Manual* (London: Open Services Project and the Joseph Rowntree Foundation).

Crouter, A. C. (1984) 'Spillover from Family to Work: The Neglected Side of the Work–Family Interface', *Human Relations*, vol. 37, no. 6, pp. 425–42.

Cupitt, S. (1997) 'Who Sets the Agenda for Empowerment?' *Breakthrough*, vol. 1, no. 2, pp. 15–28.

Dalrymple, J. and Burke, B. (1995) *Anti-oppressive Practice: Social Care and the Law* (Buckingham: Open University Press).

Davies, B. and Knapp, M. (1981) *Old People's Homes and the Production of Welfare* (London: Routledge & Kegan Paul Ltd).

Davis, A. (1996) 'Risk Work and Mental Health', in H. Kemshall and J. Pritchard (eds), *Good Practice in Risk Assessment and Risk Management* (London: Jessica Kingsley Publishers) pp. 109–20.

Department of Health (1989a) *An Introduction to The Children Act 1989* (London: HMSO).

Department of Health (1989b) *Caring for People: Community Care in the Next Decade and Beyond* (London: HMSO).

Department of Health (1990) *The Care of Children: Principles of Practice in Regulations and Guidance* (London: HMSO).

Department of Health (1991a) *Working Together under the Children Act 1989* (London: HMSO).

Department of Health (1991b) *The Children Act 1989: Guidance and Regulations, Volume 4: Residential Care* (London: HMSO).

Department of Health (1991c) *The Children Act 1989, Guidance and Regulations, Volume 3: Family Placements* (London: HMSO).

Department of Health and Welsh Office (1993) *Code of Practice: Mental Health Act 1983* (London: HMSO).

Devore, W. and Schlesinger, E. G. (1991) *Ethnic-Sensitive Social Work Practice*, 3rd edn (New York: Macmillan).

DHSS (1974) *Report of the Committee of Inquiry into the Care and Supervision Provided in Relation to Maria Colwell* (London: HMSO).

Dingwall, R. (1989) 'Some Problems about Predicting Child Abuse and Neglect', in O. Stevenson (ed.), *Child Abuse: Public Policy and Professional Practice* (Hemel Hempstead: Harvester Wheatsheaf) pp. 28–53.

Dominelli, L. (1988) *Anti-racist Social Work* (Basingstoke: Macmillan).

Dominelli, L. (1997a) *Sociology for Social Work* (Basingstoke: Macmillan).

Dominelli, L. (1997b) *Anti-racist Social Work*, 2nd edn (Basingstoke: Macmillan).

Douglas, M. (1992) *Risk and Blame: Essays in Cultural Theory* (London: Routledge).

Dowie, J. (1992a) *Professional Judgement and Decision Making D300 Volume 2 Text 6: Assessing Chances*, 3rd edn (Milton Keynes: Open University).

Dowie, J. (1992b) *Professional Judgement and Decision Making D300 Volume 2 Text 5: Structuring Decisions*, 3rd edn (Milton Keynes: Open University).

Dowie, J. (1992c) *Professional Judgement and Decision Making D300 Volume 2 Text 7: Valuing Outcomes*, 3rd edn (Milton Keynes: Open University).

Dreyfus, H. L. and Dreyfus, S. E. (1986) *Mind Over Machine: The Power of Human Intuition and Expertise in the Era of the Computer* (New York: The Free Press).

Eley, R. (1989) 'Women in Management in Social Services', in C. Hallett (ed.), *Women and Social Services Departments* (Hemel Hempstead: Harvester Wheatsheaf) pp. 155–87.

England, H. (1986) *Social Work as Art: Making Sense for Good Practice* (London: Allen & Unwin).

Etter, J. (1993) 'Levels of Co-operation and Satisfaction in 56 Open Adoptions', *Child Welfare*, vol. 72, no. 3, pp. 257–67.

Fairbairn, G. J. (1995) *Contemplating Suicide: The Language and Ethics of Self Harm* (London: Routledge).

Farmer, E. and Owen, M. (1995) *Child Protection Practice: Private Risks and Public Remedies* (London: HMSO).

Ferguson, M. (1987) 'A Feminist Interpretation of Professional Incompetence in the Beckford Case', in G. Drewry, B. Martin and B. Sheldon (eds), *After Beckford* (London: Social Policy Institute) pp. 33–9.

Fineman, S. (1995) 'Stress, Emotion and Intervention', in T. Newton with J. Handy and S. Fineman, *Managing Stress: Emotion and Power at Work* (London: Sage) pp. 120–35.

Fook, J., Ryan, M. and Hawkins, L. (1997) 'Towards a Theory of Social Work Expertise', *British Journal of Social Work*, vol. 27, pp. 399–417.

Forbes, J. and Sashidharan, S. P. (1997) 'User Involvement in Services – Incorporation or Challenge', *British Journal of Social Work*, vol. 27, pp. 481–98.

Forgas, J. P. (1995) 'Mood and Judgement: The Affect Infusion Model (AIM)', *Psychological Bulletin*, vol. 117, no. 1, pp. 39–66.

Franklin, B. and Parton, N. (1991) *Social Work, the Media and Public Relations* (London: Routledge).

Freire, P. (1972) *The Pedagogy of the Oppressed* (Harmondsworth: Penguin).

Gergen, K. J. (1985) 'The Social Constructionist Movement In Modern Psychology', *American Psychologist*, March, vol. 40, no. 3, pp. 266–75.

Gert, B. and Culver, C. M. (1979) 'The Justification of Paternalism', *Ethics*, vol. 89, pp. 199–210.

Gibbons, J., Conroy, S. and Bell, C. (1995) *Operating the Child Protection System* (London: HMSO).

Gibson, F., McGrath, A. and Reid, N. (1989) 'Occupational Stress in Social Work', *British Journal of Social Work*, vol. 19, pp. 1–16.

Goldstein, J., Freud, A. and Solnit, A. J. (1973) *Beyond the Best Interests of the Child* (New York: The Free Press).

Gorell Barnes, G. (1991) 'Ambiguities in Post-divorce Relationships' *Journal of Social Work Practice*, vol. 3, no. 2, pp. 143–50.

Greenley, R., Greenberg, J. S. and Brown, R. (1997) 'Measuring Quality of Life: A New and Practical Survey Instrument', *Social Work*, vol. 42, no. 3, pp. 244–55.

Grimwood, C. and Popplestone, R. (1993) *Women, Management and Care* (Basingstoke: Macmillan).

Hall, S. (1992) 'The New Ethnicities', in J. Donald and A. Rattansi (eds), *Race, Culture and Difference* (London: Sage) pp. 252–59.

Hallett, C. (1995) *Interagency Co-ordination in Child Protection* (London: HMSO).

Hamm, R. M. (1988) 'Clinical Intuition and Clinical Analysis: Expertise and the Cognitive Continuum', in J. Dowie and A. Elstein (eds), *Professional Judgement: A Reader in Clinical Decision Making* (Cambridge: Cambridge University Press).

Hammond, R. (1996) *Human Judgement and Social Policy: Irreducible Uncertainty, Inevitable Error, Unavoidable Injustice* (New York: Oxford University Press).

Handy, C. (1985) *Understanding Organisations*, 3rd edn (London: Penguin Books).

Hanmer, J. and Statham, D. (1988) *Women and Social Work: Towards a Women-Centred Practice* (Basingstoke: Macmillan).

Harlow, E. and Hearn, J. (1996) 'Education for Anti-Oppressive and Anti-Discriminatory Social Work Practice', *Social Work Education*, vol. 15, no. 1, pp. 5–17.

Harris, R. and Timms, R. (1993) *Secure Accommodation in Child Care: Between Hospital and Prison or Thereabouts?* (London: Routledge).

Hill, M. (1997) *The Policy Process in the Modern State*, 3rd edn (Hemel Hempstead: Prentice Hall/Harvester Wheatsheaf).

Hogarth, R. M. (1987) *Judgement and Choice: The Psychology of Decision*, 2nd edn (Chichester: John Wiley & Sons).

Hollis, M. and Howe, D. (1987) 'Moral Risks in Social Work', *Journal of Applied Philosophy*, vol. 4, no. 2, pp. 123–33.

Horne, M. (1987) *Values in Social Work* (Aldershot: Wildwood House).

Howe, D. (1992) 'Child Abuse and the Bureaucratisation of Social Work', *The Sociological Review*, vol. 40, no. 3, pp. 491–508.

Howe, D. (1994) 'Modernity, Postmodernity and Social Work', *British Journal of Social Work*, vol. 24, pp. 512–32.

Hugman, R. and Smith, D. (1995) *Ethical Issues in Social Work* (London: Routledge).

Iannello, K. P. (1992) *Decisions Without Hierarchy* (London: Routledge).

Illich, I., Zola, I. K., McKnight, J., Caplan, J. and Shaiken, H. (1977) *Disabling Professions* (New York: Marion Boyars).

Imbrogno, S. and Canada, E. (1988) 'Social Work as an Holistic System of Activity', *Social Thought*, vol. 14, Winter, pp. 12–29.

Janis, I. L. (1972) *Victims of Group Think* (New York: Harcourt Brace Jovanovich).

Janis, I. L. and Mann, L. (1977) *Decision Making: A Psychological Analysis of Conflict, Choice and Commitment* (New York: The Free Press).

Johnson, D. W. and Johnson, F. P. (1982) *Joining Together: Group Theory and Group Skills*, 2nd edn (Englewood Cliffs, New Jersey: Prentice Hall).

Johnson, T. J. (1972) *Professions and Power* (Basingstoke: Macmillan).

Jones, F., Fletcher, B. C. and Ibbetson, K. (1991) 'Stressors and Strains amongst Social Workers: Demands, Supports, Constraints, and Psychological Health', *British Journal of Social Work*, vol. 21, pp. 443–69.

Jones Finer, C. (1997) 'The New Social Policy in Britain', *Social Policy and Administration*, vol. 31, no. 5, pp. 154–70.

Kahneman, D., Slovic, P. and Tversky, A. (1982) *Judgement under Uncertainty: Heuristics and Biases* (Cambridge: Cambridge University Press).

Kempson, E. (1996) *Life on a Low Income* (York: Joseph Rowntree Foundation).

Kemshall, H. (1996) 'Offender Risk and Probation Practice', in H. Kemshall and J. Pritchard (eds), *Good Practice in Risk Assessment and Risk Management* (London: Jessica Kingsley) pp. 133–45.

Kemshall, H. and Pritchard, J. (1996) *Good Practice in Risk Assessment and Risk Management* (London: Jessica Kingsley).

La Valle, L. and Lyons, K. (1996) 'The Social Worker Speaks: 1 – Perceptions of Recent Changes in British Social Work', *Practice*, vol. 8, no. 2, pp. 5–14.

Lansdown, G. (1995) 'Children's Rights to Participation: a Critique', in C. Cloke and M. Davies (eds), *Participation and Empowerment in Child Protection* (London: Pitman Publishing) pp. 19–38.

Lazarus, R. S. (1991) *Emotion and Adaptation* (Oxford and New York: Oxford University Press).

Lazarus, R. S. and Lazarus, B. N. (1994) *Passion and Reason: Making Sense of Our Emotions* (Oxford and New York: Oxford University Press).

Leeper, R. W. (1966) 'A Critical Consideration of Egon Brunswik's Probabilistic Functionalism', in K. R. Hammond (ed.), *The Psychology of Egon Brunswik* (New York: Holt, Rinehart and Winston) pp. 405–54.

Lewis, J., Bernstock, P., Bovell, V. and Wookey, F. (1996) 'The Purchaser/ Provider Split in Social Care: Is It Working?', *Social Policy and Administration*, vol. 30, no. 1, March, pp. 1–19.

Leyens, J., Yzerbyt, V. and Schadron, G. (1994) *Stereotypes and Social Cognition* (London: Sage).

Lipsky, M. (1997) 'Street-level Bureaucracy: An Introduction', in R. Hill (ed.), *The Policy Process: A Reader*, 2nd edn (Hemel Hempstead: Prentice Hall/Harvester Wheatsheaf) pp. 389–92.

Lloyd, M. and Taylor, C. (1995) 'From Hollis to the Orange Book: Developing a Holistic Model of Social Work Assessment in the 1990s', *British Journal of Social Work*, vol. 25, 691–710.

London Borough of Greenwich (1992) *A Child in Mind: Protection of Children in a Responsible Society. The Report of the Commission of Inquiry into the Circumstances Surrounding the Death of Kimberley Carlile* (London: London Borough of Greenwich).

London Borough of Lambeth (1987) *Whose Child? The Report of the Panel Appointed to Inquire into the Death of Tyra Henry* (London: London Borough of Lambeth).

Lupton, C. (1998) 'User Empowerment or Family Self-Reliance? The Family Group Conference Model', *British Journal of Social Work*, vol. 28, pp. 107–28.

Macdonald, G. (1990) 'Allocating Blame in Social Work', *British Journal of Social Work*, vol. 20, pp. 525–46.

Mallinson, I. (1992) *The Children Act: A Social Care Guide* (London: Whiting and Birch).

Mandelstam, M. (1995) *Community Care Practice and the Law* (London: Jessica Kingsley).

Mark, J., Williams, G. and Pollock, L. R. (1993) 'Factors Mediating Suicidal Behaviour: Their Utility in Primary and Secondary Prevention' *Journal of Mental Health*, vol. 3, pp. 3–26.

Marsh, P. and Fisher, M. (1992) *Good Intentions: Developing Partnership in Social Services* (York: Joseph Rowntree Foundation).

Martinez-Brawley, E. E. and Zorita, P. M. B. (1998) 'At the Edge of the Frame: Beyond Science and Art in Social Work', *British Journal of Social Work*, vol. 28, no. 2, pp. 197–212.

McClam, T. and Woodside, M. (1994) *Problem Solving in the Helping Professions* (Pacific Grove: Brooks/Cole).

McGee, R. A. (1989) 'Burnout and Professional Decision Making: An Analogue Study', *Journal of Counselling Psychology*, vol. 36, no. 3, pp. 345–51.

Meyer, C. H. (1993) *Assessment in Social Work Practice* (New York: Columbia University Press).

Miles, R. (1989) *Racism* (London: Routledge).

Minty, T. (1995) 'Social Work's Five Deadly Sins', *Social Work and Social Sciences Review*, vol. 6, no. 1, pp. 48–63.

Modi, P., Marks, C. and Wattley, R. (1995) 'From the Margin to the Centre: Empowering the Child', in C. Cloke, and M. Davies (eds), *Participation and Empowerment in Child Protection* (London: Pitman) pp. 80–103.

Monahan, J. and Steadman, H. J. (1994) *Mental Disorder: Developments in Risk Assessment* (Chicago: University of Chicago Press).

Moore, B. (1996) *Risk Assessment: A Practitioner's Guide to Predicting Harmful Behaviour* (London: Whiting and Birch).

Morrison, C. (1988) 'Consumerism – Lessons from Community Work', *Public Administration*, vol. 66, Summer, pp. 205–14.

Morrison, T. (1993) *Staff Supervision in Social Care: An Action Learning Approach* (Harlow: Longman).

Moscovici, S. and Doise, W. (1994) *Conflict and Consensus: A General Theory of Collective Decisions* (London: Sage).

Mullaly, R. (1993) *Structural Social Work* (Toronto: McClelland and Stewart).

Mullender, A. and Ward, D. (1991) *Self-Directed Groupwork: Users Taking Action for Empowerment* (London: Whiting and Birch).

Narayan, U. (1989) 'Working Together Across Differences', in B. R. Compton and B. Galaway (eds), *Social Work Processes*, 4th edn (Belmont: Wadsworth) pp. 317–28.

Nocon, A. and Qureshi, H. (1996) *Outcomes of Community Care for Users and Carers* (Buckingham: Open University Press).

Norris, D. (1990) *Violence Against Social Workers: The Implication for Practice* (London: Jessica Kingsley Publishers).

O'Sullivan, T. (1988) 'Simulation Games and Social Work Education: The Woods Family, A Problem-Solving and Decision-Making Game for Social Workers', *Social Work Education*, vol. 7, no. 3, Summer, pp. 12–16.

O'Sullivan, T. (1990) 'Responding to People with Dementia', *Practice*, vol. 4, no. 1, pp. 5–15.

O'Sullivan, T. (1994) *Social Work with and within Groups, Unit 3: Working with Family Groups* (London: Open Learning Foundation).

Oatley, R. and Jenkins, J. M. (1996) *Understanding Emotions* (Cambridge, Mass.: Blackwell) .

Oliver, J. (1991) 'The Social Care Directive: Development of a Quality of Life Profile for Use in Community Services for the Mentally Ill', *Social Work and Social Services Review*, vol. 3, pp. 5–45.

Otway, O. (1996) 'Social Work with Children and Families: From Child Welfare to Child Protection', in N. Parton (ed.), *Social Theory, Social Change and Social Work* (London: Routledge) pp. 152–71.

Øvretveit, J. (1993) *Co-ordinating Community Care: Multi-disciplinary Teams and Care Management* (Buckingham: Open University Press).

Pahl, J. (1994) '"Like the Job – but Hate the Organisation": Social Workers and Managers in Social Services', in R. Page and J. Baldock (eds), *Social Policy Review 6* (Canterbury: Social Policy Association).

Parker, R., Ward, H., Jackson, S., Aldgate, J. and Wedge, P. (1991) *Assessing Outcomes in Child Care* (London: HMSO).

Parry, N., Rustin, M. and Satyamurti, C. (eds) (1979) *Social Work Welfare and the State* (London: Edward Arnold).

Parton, N. (1996) 'Social Work, Risk and "The Blaming System"', in N. Parton (ed.), *Social Theory, Social Change and Social Work* (London: Routledge) pp. 98–114.

Parton, N. (1998) 'Risk, Advanced Liberalism and Child Welfare: The Need to Rediscover Uncertainty and Ambiguity', *British Journal of Social Work*, vol. 28, pp. 5–27.

Patel, N. (1990) *A 'Race' Against Time?: Social Services Provision to Black Elders* (London: Runnymede Trust).

Payne, M. (1989) 'Open Records and Shared Decisions with Clients', in Steven Shardlow (ed.), *The Values of Change in Social Work* (London: Tavistock/Routledge) pp. 114–35.

Payne, M. (1994) 'Personal Supervision in Social Work', in A. Connor and S. Black (eds), *Performance Review and Quality in Social Work* (London: Jessica Kingsley) pp. 43–58.

Payne, M. (1996) *What is Professional Social Work?* (Birmingham: Venture Press).

Payne, M. (1997a) 'Government Guidance in the Construction of the Social Work Profession' in R. Adams (ed.), *Crisis in the Human Services: National and International Issues* (Kingston upon Hull: University of Lincolnshire and Humberside) pp. 381–90.

Payne, M. (1997b) *Modern Social Work Theory: A Critical Introduction*, 2nd edn (Basingstoke: Macmillan).

Penfold, P. S. and Walker, G. A. (1984) *Women and the Psychiatric Paradox* (Milton Keynes: Open University Press).

Penhale, B. (1992) 'Decision-Making and Mental Incapacity: Practice Issues for Professionals', *Practice*, vol. 5, no. 3, pp. 186–95.

Penhale, B. (1993) 'The Abuse of Elderly People: Considerations for Practice', *British Journal of Social Work*, vol. 23, no. 2, pp. 95–112.

Phillipson, J. (1992) *Practising Equality: Women, Men and Social Work* (London: CCETSW).

Pugh, R. (1996) *Effective Language in Health and Social Work* (London: Chapman & Hall).

Radford, K. J. (1989) *Individual and Small Group Decisions* (New York: Springer-Verlag Captus University Publications).

Reamer, F. G. (1995) *Social Work Values and Ethics* (New York: Columbia University Press).

Reder, P., Duncan, S. and Gray, M. (1993) *Beyond Blame: Child Abuse Tragedies Revisited* (London: Routledge).

Rees, S. (1991) *Achieving Power: Practice and Policy in Social Welfare* (St Leonards, Australia: Allen & Unwin).

Rhodes, M. L. (1985) 'Gilligan's Theory of Moral Developments as Applied to Social Work', *Social Work*, March-April, pp. 101–5.

Rhodes, M. L. (1986) *Ethical Dilemmas in Social Work Practice* (Boston, Mass.: Routledge and Kegan Paul).

Rojek, C. and Collins, S. A. (1987) 'Contract or Con Trick', *British Journal of Social Work*, vol. 17, pp. 199–211.

Satyamurti, C. (1981) *Occupational Survival: The Case of the Local Authority Social Worker* (Oxford: Basil Blackwell).

Schein, E. H. (1988) *Process Consultation: Volume 1, Its Role in Organisation Development* (Reading, Mass.: Addison-Wesley).

Schon, D. A. (1995) *The Reflective Practitioner: How Professionals Think in Action* (Aldershot: Arena).

Scott, D. (1998) 'A Qualitative Study of Social Work Assessment in Cases of Alleged Child Abuse', *British Journal of Social Work*, vol. 28, pp. 73–88.

Scutt, N. (1995) 'Child Advocacy: Getting the Child's Voice Heard', in C. Cloke and M. Davies (eds), *Participation and Empowerment in Child Protection* (London: Pitman).

Seed, P. and Lloyd, G. (1997) *Quality of Life* (London: Jessica Kingsley).

Sheppard, M. (1990) *Mental Health, The Role of the Approved Social Worker* (Sheffield: Joint Unit for Social Services Research).

Sheppard, M. (1995a) 'Social Work, Social Science and Practice Wisdom', *British Journal of Social Work*, vol. 25, pp. 265–93.

Sheppard, M. (1995b) *Care Management and the New Social Work: A Critical Analysis* (London: Whiting and Birch).

Sibeon, R. (1990) 'Comments on the Structure and Forms of Social Work Knowledge', *Social Work and Social Sciences Review*, vol. 1, no. 1, pp. 29–44.

Sinclair, I. (ed.) (1988) *Residential Care: The Research Reviewed* (London: HMSO).

Singh, G. (1996) 'Promoting Anti-Racist and Black Perspectives in Social Work Education and Practice Teaching', *Social Work Education*, vol. 15, no. 2, pp. 35–57.

Smith, M. G. (1986) 'Pluralism, Race and Ethnicity in Selected African Countries', in J. Rex and D. Mason (eds), *Theories of Race and Ethnic Relations* (Cambridge: Cambridge University Press) pp. 187–225.

Social Services Inspectorate/Social Work Services Group (1991) *Care Management and Assessment Practitioners' Guide* (London: HMSO).

Spicker, P. (1990) 'Social Work and Self-determination', *British Journal of Social Work*, vol. 20, pp. 221–36.

Spinelli, E. (1989) *The Interpreted World: An Introduction to Phenomenological Psychology* (London: Sage).

Stanley, N. and Manthorpe, J. (1997) 'Risk Assessment: Developing Training for Professionals in Mental Health Work', *Social Work and Social Sciences Review*, vol. 7, no. 1, pp. 26–38.

Stevenson, O. (1986) 'Guest Editorial on the Jasmine Beckford Inquiry', *British Journal of Social Work*, vol. 16, no. 5, pp. 501–10.

Stevenson, O. (1989) 'Multi-disciplinary Work', in O. Stevenson (ed.), *Child Abuse: Public Policy and Professional Practice* (Hemel Hempstead: Wheatsheaf) pp. 173–203.

Strachan, R. (1997) 'Improving Judgement and Appreciating Biases within the Risk Assessment Process', in H. Kemshall, and J. Pritchard (eds), *Good Practice in Risk Assessment and Risk Management 2: Protection, Rights and Responsibilities* (London: Jessica Kingsley) pp. 15–26.

Tanner, D. (1998) 'The Jeopardy of Risk', *Practice*, vol. 10, no. 1, pp. 15–28.

Tetlock, P. E. (1985) 'Accountability: The Neglected Social Context of Judgement and Choice', *Research in Organisation Behaviour*, vol. 7, pp. 297–332.

Thoburn, J., Lewis, A. and Shemmings, D. (1995) *Paternalism or Partnership? Family Involvement in the Child Protection Process* (London: HMSO).

Thomas, M. and Pierson, J. (1997) *Dictionary of Social Work* (London: Collins).

Thompson, N. (1996) *People Skills: A Guide to Effective Practice in the Human Services* (Basingstoke: Macmillan).

Thompson, N. (1997) *Anti-Discriminatory Practice*, 2nd edn (Basingstoke: Macmillan).

Thompson, N., Murphy, M. and Stradling, S. (1994) *Dealing with Stress* (Basingstoke: Macmillan).

Thompson, N., Stradling, S., Murphy, M. and O'Neill, P. (1996) 'Stress and Organisational Culture', *British Journal of Social Work*, vol. 26, pp. 647–65.

Vernon, S. (1990) *Social Work and the Law* (London: Butterworths).

Vroom, V. H. and Jago, A. G. (1988) *The New Leadership: Managing Participation in Organisations* (Englewood Cliffs, New Jersey: Prentice Hall).

Wald, M. S. and Woolverton, M. (1990) 'Risk Assessment: The Emperor's New Clothes', *Child Welfare*, vol. 69, pp. 483–511.

Wattam, C. (1995) 'The Investigative Process' in K. Wilson and A. James (eds), *The Child Protection Handbook* (London: Baillière Tindall) pp. 170–187.

Webb, S. W. (1994) '"My Client is Subversive": Partnership and Patronage in Social Work', *Social Work and Social Sciences Review*, vol. 5, no. 1, pp. 5–23.

Wetherly, P. (1996) 'Basic Need and Social Policies', *Critical Social Policy*, vol. 16, pp. 45–65.

Williams, R. (1981) *Culture* (London: Fontana).

Woodhouse, D. and Pengelly, P. (1991) *Anxiety and the Dynamics of Collaboration* (Aberdeen: Aberdeen University Press).

Wright, K., Haycox, A. and Leedham, I. (1994) *Evaluating Community Care: Services for People with Learning Difficulties* (Buckingham: Open University Press).

Zey, M. (1992) *Decision Making: Alternatives to Rational Choice Models* (Newbury Park: Sage).

Author Index

Subject Index

192